A THEATRE FOR ALL SEASONS

The History of the Everyman Theatre,
Cheltenham

Michael Hasted

with a foreword by Steven Berkoff

Northern Arts Publications

Published by Northern Arts Publications
an imprint of Jeremy Mills Publishing Limited
www.jeremymillspublishing.co.uk

First published 2011
Text © Michael Hasted 2011
Images © as attributed

The moral right of Michael Hasted to be identified as the author of this work has been asserted.

All rights reserved. No part of this book may be reproduced in any form or by any means without prior permission in writing from the publisher.

ISBN   Paperback 978-1-906600-60-0
        Hardback 978-1-906600-61-7

Cover Image
The auditorium of the Everyman Theatre.
Photo Michael Hasted

Contents

Foreword by Steven Berkoff — vii

Chapter 1
George III and Piggy Ninny — 1
Theatre in Cheltenham prior to the Opera House

Chapter 2
Vestibules and Sloat Sliders — 13
Cheltenham has a brand new theatre

Chapter 3
Jersey Lily and Lillah on a chair — 21
The best show in town as the new theatre opens

Chapter 4
The future looks bright — 29
The early years 1900-1918

Chapter 5
A mauve dress and the Northwest Frontier — 37
The theatre between the wars

Chapter 6
Twinkle and a Naughty Cat — 47
The Opera House at war 1939-1945

Chapter 7
Pantos and Panties — 55
The end of the Opera House 1946-1959

Chapter 8
Everyman for himself — 67
A new era in Regent Street 1959-1961

Chapter 9 — 81
YEG, ETA, CODS & GCHQ
Lots of initial support

Chapter 10 — 89
Hay Days and Salad Days
The future's bright, the future's yellow 1961–1971

Chapter 11 — 105
Purple Haze
The Malcolm Farquhar years 1971–1983

Chapter 12 — 119
Things that go bump in the night…
Spooky things and strange phenomena

Chapter 13 — 127
Out, out brief candle
The Everyman is re-built 1983–1986

Chapter 14 — 135
The Winds of Change
The final years of the rep 1986–1995

Chapter 15 — 153
For what we are about to receive
The Everyman as a receiving theatre

Chapter 16 — 165
The cherubs smile again
The Everyman is restored to its former glory

Acknowledgements — 173
Notes — 174
List of managers/artistic directors — 175
Glossary of Theatre Terms — 176
Map — 178
Index — 179

Foreword by Steven Berkoff

How can it be 50 years since I set foot on the Everyman Theatre stage for the first time? Yet it is, and to the very month.

Though still an uncouth and untried actor I was cast by David Giles in his first season as a director of that lovely theatre and I was so grateful to him since he only interviewed me and didn't require me to audition. He just chatted to me and must have been so struck by my utter enthusiasm that he cast me as Oberon, the king of the fairies in *Midsummer Night's Dream*. God, was I overwhelmed when I heard the news from him on the phone. I actually remember rolling around the floor in excitement.

For my 'Puck', Giles cast an extraordinary actor called Tony Tanner who, like his name was bright, glittering and rather brilliant. Frankly at the time I had never seen anyone quite like him and I must say I was somewhat in awe, as in fact we all were.

Though nervous as hell I made the role my own and got through as best I could. I also recall Windsor Davies who later found TV fame and joined the acting profession late in his life and was not too modest to be an assistant stage manager. He was so excited to be in the magical mystical world of theatre that he beamed from morning to night.

The theatre seems light and airy and pleasant to work in and I had some lovely digs just down the road and since it was a small flat I cooked for myself and just loved sitting in my own kitchen which was so bright and sunny. I got through the *Dream* and then was cast in Henry James' *The Aspern Papers* beautifully adapted by the late Michael Redgrave. Fortunately I had seen the West End production with Redgrave himself and the legendary actress Beatrix Lehmann, who had such an almost hypnotic power with her words.

However, I recall most vividly the actor playing Pasqual, whom I was cast for. He was simply phenomenal and moved like an animal: graceful, strutting, alert. I had his performance fixed firmly in my mind and so when I rehearsed I couldn't have had a better example to have worked for and my Pasquale was well reviewed. The skilled and suave actor Peter Brett played the lead and was excellent. Ah yes! The actor's name was Olaf Pooley who struck me so forcibly. God, there were great actors in those days!

So my reputation increased measurably after that part and I started to rate myself a little higher as an actor. Then we did a sentimental American comedy called *The Matchmaker* which was a charming piece of twaddle and made a good impression on the audience, and as I remember was beautifully designed by Kenneth Mellor.

An older actor, Clifford Parish, was one of the lads and was a most supportive chap. We remained friends well after the season ended. I let myself down rather badly in the fifth show I did which was written by Tony Tanner and his partner, the composer Neville Morgan. I really couldn't sing and at the interview when Giles seemed so taken with me it was one of the questions he had asked, and of course like all young actors begging for work, you admit to doing everything. And now I was to be tested.

Neville McGrah was one of the nicest, gentlest, sweetest men I had ever met. He was so very patient with me when going over my few songs and was so encouraging and never for a moment critical of my poor efforts. In the end I was only miserably cast as the Town Crier, but still had to sing it and the song remains in my mind to this day. Of course it was a vehicle for Tanner and he carried it off superbly. I think Tony as the writer was a tad or more disappointed with me and from thence he certainly had little time for me. I did meet David Giles again since he was employed as a dialogue coach on the epic movie *Nicholas and Alexander*.

Cheltenham to me was the summer of my life and I don't think I can ever forget it. I remember hiring a bike and on Sundays, taking myself off for long rides into the beautiful countryside. There's so much else I could say and remember but for now I am sure that this will do.

God bless The Everyman, you are forever in my heart.

Steven Berkoff,
London, May 2011

*To Astrid,
for everything,
as always.*

THEATRE,
ROYAL OLD WELLS.
ENTHUSIASTIC RECEPTION
OF THE DRURY-LANE ENGLISH

OPERA COMPANY!
COMPRISING THE FOLLOWING CELEBRATED ARTISTES:

Miss JULIA HARLAND
Miss FANNY REEVES
Mr. HENRY CORRI
Mr. J. GLENVILLE
Mr. D'ARCY READ
Mr. ELLIOT GALER
(THE NEW ENGLISH TENOR), AND
MR. LINDLEY NORMAN,
(CONDUCTOR).

Tuesday, May 15, 1855,
The Performance will commence with Bellini's popular Opera, of

LA SONNAMBULA

Amina	Miss JULIA HARLAND
Liza	Miss FANNY REEVES
Theresa	Miss HODSON
Count Rodolpho	Mr. HENRY CORRI
Elvino	Mr. ELLIOT GALER
Alessio	Mr. J. GLENVILLE
The Notary .. Mr. MORGAN Postillion .. Mr. REID Servant .. Mr. PENDEGRASS	

INCIDENTAL TO THE OPERA THE FOLLOWING MUSIC—

ACT I.

Introduction and Chorus—"Viva! Viva!"
Air—"Sounds so joyful," .. .. .. Miss Fanny Reeves
Recitative—"Dearest Companions," .. Miss Julia Harland
Air—"O, Love! for me thy power," .. Miss Julia Harland
Chorus—"Fortune around Amina,"
Cavatina—"While this heart," .. .. Miss Julia Harland
Duet—"Take now this ring," Miss Julia Harland & Mr Elliot Galer
Chorus—"Ah! who can this be?"
Recitativo—"Yes, the Mill," .. .. .. Mr. Henry Corri
Air—"As I view these scenes," .. .. Mr. Henry Corri
Air—"Maid, those bright eyes," .. .. Mr. Henry Corri
Celebrated Spectre Chorus—"When daylight's going,"
Recitative—"But from my toilsome journey," .. Mr. Henry Corri
Chorus—"Good repose."

ACT II.

Recitative—"Good Heavens!" .. .. Mr. Henry Corri
Recitative—"Thou'rt jealous of thy Amina," Miss Julia Harland
Duet—"O Heaven! tempt me not,"Miss Julia Harland & Mr. E. Galer
Chorus—"What a curious, strange adventure."
Recitative—"Thou speakest falsely," .. Mr. Elliot Galer
Recitative—"Ah! where am I?" .. Miss Julia Harland
Chorus—"Let this confound thee."
Recitative—"Unhappy maiden," .. .. Miss Julia Harland
Concerted Piece—"Hear me swear, then," Miss Julia Harland
Miss Fanny Reeves, Mr. Elliot Galer, and Chorus.
Recitative—"Now avoid thee," .. .. Mr. Elliot Galer
Duet and Chorus—"Such return for love," Miss Julia Harland and Mr. Elliot Galer
Grand Chorus—"Let her bear her crimes afar,".. Characters

ACT III.

Recitative—"See him, dear mother," .. Miss Julia Harland
Grand Scena—"All is lost," .. .. .. Mr. Elliot Galer
Recitative—"Ah! this is cruel," .. .. Miss Julia Harland
Cavatina—"Still so gently," .. .. .. Mr. Elliot Galer
Quartette and Chorus—"If I saw it, I could believe it," Miss F. Reeves Mr. Elliot Galer and Mr. Henry Corri
Chorus—"Hear us, kind heaven."
Chorus—"She's saved, she's saved." .. Miss Julia Harland
Recitative—"Once could I but see him," .. Mr. Henry Corri
"Hear me, she's dreaming," Miss Fanny Reeves
"Speaking of thee," Miss Julia Harland
"'Tis hoping vainly," Miss Julia Harland
Grand Finale—"Ah! do not mingle,".. Miss Julia Harland and all the Characters.

To conclude with the Musical Farce of THE

LOAN OF A LOVER!

Captain Amersfort,	Mr. D'ARCY READ
Peter Spyk,	Mr. J. GLENVILLE
Swyzel, .. Mr. MORGAN Delve,	Mr. PENDEGRASS
Gertrude, with Songs,	Miss FANNY REEVES
Ernestine,	Miss HODSON

Chapter 1

George III and Piggy Ninny
Theatre in Cheltenham prior to the Opera House

Not much happened on 1st October 1891. Nobody famous was born on that day – unless of course you include cricketer Ralph du Boulay Evans – and nobody famous died. No great battles took place and no great laws were passed. No great ocean liners sank and the best the *Echo* could report was that a farmer on Cleeve Hill had lost some sheep. Queen Victoria had been on the throne for 54 years and the British Prime Minister was Robert Gascoyne-Cecil, Marquis of Salisbury.

But there were quite a few people who had marked that otherwise insignificant day in their diaries. Lillie Langtry, the country's most famous actress, was one. Others included the dignitaries, lords, ladies and high society of Cheltenham Spa in the county of Gloucestershire.

The event that everybody had been so eagerly awaiting since the previous spring finally arrived with the grand opening of the New Theatre and Opera House. At twenty-past-seven that Thursday evening about one thousand people witnessed the building receiving 'a baptism of light' when 30 incandescent lamps enclosed in pearl-like globes were switched on. Cheltenham had a brand new theatre, continuing a line of theatrical history in the town which went back nearly four hundred years.

The earliest recorded public entertainment in Cheltenham was in 1611 when a certain Guy Dobbins marched through town, banging a drum to the delight of a noisy crowd. Cheltenham at the time was little more than the High Street, which ran for about a mile east to west with the Parish Church at its centre. The rest of the town consisted of a tangle of dark, narrow passages leading off the High Street.

Prancing alongside Mr. Dobbins was Richard Clarke brandishing a truncheon, pretending to be an officer of the law. They were advertising a play scheduled to take place at The Crown tavern that evening but they were waylaid by the local bailiff before they got very far. Fearing the spread of the plague which was already infecting nearby Tredington and Prestbury, the bailiff proceeded to The Crown where inn-keeper Thomas Milton was ordered to cancel the performance.[1]

By the middle of the eighteenth century Cheltenham was very much on the circuit for itinerant theatre companies. *The Cirencester Flying Post* announced a visit to the town in August 1744 of the Warwick Company of Comedians who would be 'entertaining the quality and gentry there.'[2] In July 1758 Mr. William's Company of Comedians was in town to give three performances.[3]

It seems one of the first places in the town that could claim to be an actual theatre was a converted malt house. The humble out-building was part of Newcastle House, a lodging house in Coffee House Lane which is now Pittville Street.

In about 1773 the malt house was sold to John Boles Watson, a member of a wealthy Irish Quaker family. Watson was described in 1796 by the actor Michael Kelly as 'a fellow of infinite jest and humour; full of Thespian anecdotes, and perfect master of the art of driving away wreathed melancholy. Many a hearty laugh I had with him: he was an Irishman and had, although I say it who should not say it, all the natural wit of his country about him ...'[4]

The Coffee House Yard Theatre, as it became known, was primitive in the extreme being little more that a shed with straw covering the floor. Nevertheless, Sarah Siddons, the greatest actress of her generation was to play there, as did her brother John Phillip Kemble. In fact, this was said to be Kemble's first appearance on any stage.

There is a passage in the 1856 novel *John Halifax, Gentleman* by Dinah Craik that describes the theatre and its rowdy audiences. 'In a few minutes we had started in a flutter of gaiety and excitement for Coffee House Yard Theatre. It was a poor place, little better than a barn, built in the lane leading out of the High Street. This lane was almost blocked up with play-goers of all ranks, and in all sorts of equipages, from the coach to the sedan chair, mingled with a motley crowd on foot all jostling, fighting and screaming, till the place became a complete bear garden …'

Lord Ailesbury, who had seen Siddons in a show there, mentioned her to David Garrick, the greatest actor-manager of his day, who ran the Drury Lane Theatre in London. Garrick sent an envoy, a Mr. King, to Cheltenham to see her in a play called *The Fair Penitent*. Siddons later wrote, 'I knew neither Mr King nor his purpose, but I shortly afterwards received an offer from Garrick himself, upon very low terms. Happy to be placed where I presumptuously argued that I should do all that I have since achieved, if I could but once gain the opportunity, I instantly paid my respects to the great man. I was at that time good-looking; and certainly, all things considered, an actress well worthy my poor five pounds per week.'

Soon after Siddons' first appearance, the old theatre was extended and improvements were made. *The Cheltenham Guide* from 1780 described the changes. 'The Old Play House, which has lately been fitted up and beautified, is neat, but not sufficiently spacious to seat a large audience, so that on particular nights many are obliged to forego the amusement of the theatre. Plays are here acted thrice a week, Tuesday, Thursday and Saturday, during the season by a Company of Comedians, chiefly from Worcester; who, without aiming at elegance of scenery and decorations, exert their best endeavours to deserve approbation, and accordingly meet with encouragement. The subscription is a guinea for eighteen nights, or two shillings the Pit, and one shilling the Gallery, each evening. It has been proposed to form a Committee of Gentlemen, and erect a new and commodious theatre by subscriptions; each subscriber to receive a proportionable share of the net rent according to his deposit.'

By this time John Boles Watson was running theatres in Gloucester, Bristol, Cirencester, Tewkesbury and Stroud. In 1782 he established Cheltenham's first purpose-built theatre, a few yards from the eastern end of the High Street in York Passage which led to what is now Grosvenor Terrace.

On 12th July 1788 King George III arrived in Cheltenham to take the waters. He was to stay nearly five weeks. During his visit he, along with the Queen and other courtiers, made regular visits to Watson's theatre, thereby entitling it, by letters patent, to be called the Theatre Royal.

On the evening of 24th July the Royal party visited the theatre to see Mrs. Jordan play Rosalind in *As You Like It*, attended by 'the most elegant and numerous audience ever known in Cheltenham. About two hundred and eighty were turned back from the boxes only. The scenes were crowded ... and the applause was great. Rosalind was given

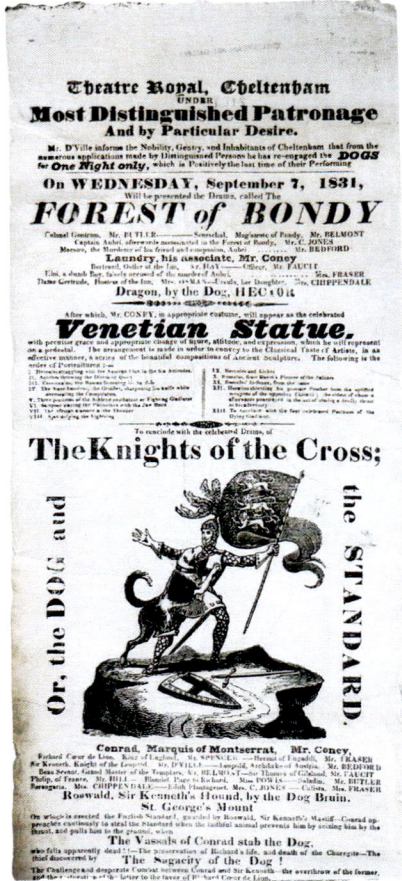

Poster courtesy of Cheltenham Museum and Art Gallery

Grosvenor Passage, site of the original Theatre Royal.

photos: Michael Hasted

with much arch playfulness and the serious passages were delivered in a manner that astonished all present'.[5]

Overnight the King's visit transformed Cheltenham into one of the most fashionable and exciting towns in England. The court, which accompanied the King, was very impressed with Watson's theatre, one of them noting, 'The scenery and machinery were prepared at the Royalty Theatre. Mr Penn's *Don Juan* deserved the encomiums of the whole house, and Mr Kelly, brother to the gentleman of the same name at Drury Lane, pleased much in a soft song. Mr Kelly copies his brother with great exactness. Signor Rossignol is here and at Mr Watson's dinner yesterday performed a solo on the poker with great wit and humour. The theatre is a very elegant and commodious structure, erected by Mr Watson, the proprietor and manager. There are two rows of boxes, one in the form of a gallery, behind which in a most ingenious manner is erected another gallery for the servants, etc. The whole of the theatre, scenery, etc. is above mediocrity and the performers are equal to the task of doing their parts justice'.[6]

The Royal Party left Cheltenham on 16th August and on the night before their departure attended a gala performance at the theatre. The upper boxes were crowded with all the fashion that Gloucester, Worcester and the county could send.[7] The playbills for the evening were printed on white satin.

The cramped York Passage building soon became too small to accommodate the enthusiastic and growing audiences and Watson needed to expand. He bought some land just a couple of hundred yards away in the newly fashionable Cambray on the other side of the High Street and built his new theatre there at a cost of £8,000. The new, grander Theatre Royal opened in 1805 in Cambray Meadows, site of the current Bath Street.

The new theatre was patronised by the great and the good who were now flocking to Cheltenham. The town was visited by the Duke of Wellington, Lord Byron and, in 1816, Jane Austen. Jane came with her sister Cassandra to take the waters. They stayed at Mrs. Potter's lodgings in the High Street next door to the original Theatre Royal which had by then been absorbed into the York Hotel.

Perhaps the most famous artist to appear at the theatre was the clown Joseph Grimaldi. His father, Signor Giuseppe or Joseph 'Iron Legs' Grimaldi, was an Italian pantomime and circus artist and ballet-master at Drury Lane. His mother was Rebecca Brooker, a dancer in the theatre's *corps de ballet*. Born in Clare Market, Grimaldi made his first appearance at nearby Drury Lane when less than two-years-old and by the age of three, he was appearing at Sadler's Wells.

Joseph Grimaldi

Grimaldi was popular in Cheltenham right up until his death and in his later years was supported by local *bon viveur*, Colonel Berkeley and Lord Byron who organised three separate visits to the town for *The Prince of Clowns* between 1812 and 1823. For his final visit he was in poor health but was temporarily revitalised by taking the waters. He dined with the Colonel at his home at Berkeley Castle and later with Byron. Grimaldi's three visits grossed £530, of which he received half.[8]

Samuel Seward, a scenery painter at the Theatre Royal, ran his own puppet theatre in St. George's Place. He named it Sadlers Wells after the theatre in London where he had once worked. His productions were as spectacular as anything that the Theatre Royal could offer except they didn't have live actors. The theatre performed continuously for thirty years until the death of Seward and his wife. Mr. Belmont of the Theatre Royal took over the theatre replacing puppets with live actors and renaming it the New Clarence Theatre. The new venture was not a great success and closed in the 1830s, becoming Gardner's Academy, a private seminary owned by Joseph Gardner. The Church of England Reading Association took it over and ironically it was Francis Close, who was so opposed to most forms of entertainment, particularly the theatre, who inaugurated it in 1839.[9]

During work on the St. George's Place building in the 1970s the façade, including the original sign for the theatre, was discovered. At the time it was thought to be the oldest surviving puppet theatre in the country. It was subsequently demolished and no trace remains.

The Theatre Royal and Mr. Watson had a virtual monopoly in Cheltenham for public entertainment, but with Watson's death in March 1813 and the theatre's waning popularity, another venue a hundred yards along the High Street, was keen to offer an alternative.

The new Assembly Rooms, which re-opened on 29th July 1816, while not in direct competition with the town's theatre, were now in the ascendancy as the Theatre Royal declined. The opening coincided with the visit of the nation's hero, the Duke of Wellington.

The Assembly Rooms, on the corner of the High Street and Rodney Road, a site now occupied by Lloyds Bank, soon became the social hub of the town, hosting balls, concerts and other public events and was very much the 'in' place for the town's high society. In fact, they were very choosy as to who they let in. A new rule in 1826 ironically stated that, '… no theatrical or other performers by profession be admitted.'

To coincide with the first meeting at the new Prestbury racecourse on 17th July 1831, Signor Niccolò Paganini was in town to give two sell-out concerts at the Assembly Rooms, one on the Wednesday evening, the 20th, followed by a second on the following Thursday afternoon. Nearly eight hundred spectators crowded into the hall for each concert.[10]

Not to be outdone, Mr. DeVille, who was then the proprietor of the Theatre Royal, pulled off a major coup when he hurried along to the Plough Hotel, where the maestro was staying, and persuaded him to give a third concert at his venue. This would be for 'the lower classes' who would not have been able to afford the extravagant affair just around the corner.

In spite of all of DeVille's frantic efforts to drum up an audience in the few hours available to him, at the appointed hour not enough people had turned up at the theatre to cover Paganini's agreed fee and he refused to play. The crowd got angry and marched along the High Street to the Plough chanting 'Piggy Ninny, Piggy Ninny'.

The violinist was persuaded to change his mind and even waived his fee, saying it should be given to Cheltenham's poor. However, it soon became clear that the mob in the street were not in fact people who had bought tickets for the Theatre Royal, but just a rowdy mob. Paganini was not pleased and as soon as the concert was over he hastily left town on the eleven-thirty *post-chaise* to London.[11]

The sad and sorry end to the Theatre Royal came on 3rd May 1839 when the building was completely destroyed by fire. It was to be another fifty-two years before Cheltenham was to have another proper, purpose-built theatre.

The theatrical void was not helped by a wave of puritanism that was sweeping the town. Public entertainment by this time had come up against the formidable Rev. Francis Close, a fervent Evangelist who had been appointed curate in charge of the Parish Church in 1826. In 1827, during race week, Close launched his campaign against it, preaching a sermon entitled *On the Evil Consequences of Attending the Racecourse*. When the Theatre Royal went up in flames Close decreed that no regular theatre was to be established in Cheltenham while he remained in the town. His main adversary was local playboy Colonel Berkeley, a man who was involved in most aspects of entertainment and debauchery in the town.

The Assembly Rooms

In 1850, at the height of the Evangelical movement, Close delivered a sermon entitled *The Tendencies of the Stage, Religion and Moral*, but not everybody took him seriously. A popular rhyme that could be heard in the streets of Cheltenham at the time went:

> *And if you to the Playhouse get*
> *Old Nick will know it, for he'll set*
> *Old Close to watch your motions.*

However, a new theatre was created without anyone really noticing on the site of the Royal Old Well in the Montpellier part of town. George Rowe, a printer and artist, along with architect Samuel Onley launched their cunning plan in 1838 when they inaugurated an event to establish their enterprise under the pretext of creating a new spa. After buying the remaining part of the old Well Walk area they proceeded to build a new hall to house the spa, promising a place for 'respectable amusements.' Incidentally, the house that Onley built for himself at the top of Bayshill Road is now the Montpellier Chapter Hotel.

The third Old Well Pump Room was finally opened on 20th June 1850 with a hugely successful Grand Horticultural Exhibition. However, immediately afterwards the building was renamed the Royal Well Music Hall and had a proscenium and flying system installed. Rowe and Onley had surreptitiously built a new theatre in Cheltenham

Niccolo Paganini

Opening of the New Royal Well in 1850
Courtesy of Kath Boothman

Interior of the New Royal Well
Courtesy of Cheltenham Ladies College

right under the nose of the Reverend Close. Probably to Close's glee and possibly because of his influence, the new theatre was not a great success and the partnership broke up after one more season, with Onley retaining the building. Their failure was partly attributed to the Great Exhibition which was running that year and for a while the theatre reverted to its previous uses.

At some point Onley re-opened the building as The Theatre Royal and installed a horse-shoe shaped gallery as well as a sixpenny upper gallery and blacked out the windows with paint.

The Reverend Close is generally blamed for sounding Cheltenham's death knell by finally managing to ban all theatres and the race meetings. Despite Close's objection to the theatre and entertainment on religious and moral grounds, the Salvation Army was more pragmatic. St. Peter's Hall had been built for them in 1849 by the old gas works at the beginning of Tewkesbury Road. Situated in a part of town then known as Lower Dockem, the hall was

not popular so they started looking for somewhere else. They rented the new Royal Well Theatre for Sunday afternoons for a short time until another hall became available in the Bath Road. The venue, The Colosseum, had been called the Wellington Hall and seated about 1,200 people. This was frequently used for circuses and was often referred to as 'the circus.'[12] The site is used by the Salvation Army to this day.

John Neville Maskelyne

Pantomimes were regularly performed at the Royal Well but their suitability for children was in some doubt. William Thomas Swift, a school-master at Badgeworth, near Gloucester, recorded in his diary going to see the pantomime on Boxing Day, 1871. He noted that the performance was spoiled by the stench and row; the gallery was crowded and amidst the coarse remarks and swearing it was almost impossible to hear the show. Swift also mentions going to the theatre in 1884 and seeing *The Three Hats* which was enlivened towards the end by the arrival of Lord Fitzhardinge who received an ovation. However, it was Yeomanry Week and the Promenade was over-run by a good many Hussars 'giggling and strutting – some rather broad in their pronunciation'.[13]

The Ladies' College took over the lease of the theatre in 1887, finally buying it outright in 1890.[14] The theatre was demolished and The Princess Hall was built on the site in 1897, where it still stands today.

John Nevil Maskelyne, one of the foremost illusionists of his time, was born in White Hart Row, now Whitehart Street, in Cheltenham in 1839. He became a watchmaker with a shop in Montpellier, a few yards up the hill from the Royal Well. His first performance was at Cheltenham's old town hall, just along the road from the current theatre. In 1873 he and his partner, George Cooke, opened a permanent theatre/exhibition; *Maskelyne and Cooke's Magic House of Mystery*, in part of the Egyptian Hall in London's Piccadilly. Maskelyne's grandson, Jasper, would appear at the Opera House in 1939.

William Charles Macready, the classical actor and friend of Charles Dickens, appeared in Cheltenham on several occasions. In 1825 the *Cheltenham Chronicle* wrote, 'Mr. Macready's *Virginius* stands alone in the solitary pre-eminence of genius. It is perfect. Acting cannot go beyond it. No acting of his that we have lately seen can approach it'.

Top: The High Street at The Plough Hotel with the Assembly Rooms in the distance.

Bottom: The Egyptian Hall, London
Both pictures courtesy of Sue Rowbotham

The Winter Gardens in Imperial Square in 1906

Macready retired to Cheltenham in 1860 and died at his house at 6, Wellington Square on 27th April 1873, aged eighty.

The final place of entertainment to be established in Cheltenham prior to the Opera House was The Winter Gardens which opened in 1878 in Imperial Square. The plan was for the south wing to be used as a roller-skating rink and the other to be used as a concert hall. It was clearly not a very good plan. The hall was cold and draughty and the noise of rain falling on the glass roof made performances unfeasible, while the glass walls were so thin that the music could be clearly heard outside. Many people who lived nearby preferred to stay in their own home to listen to the music emanating from the hall rather than buy tickets.[15]

When the Royal Well Theatre closed in 1887 the Assembly Rooms became the only venue of any note, but within a few weeks they were seriously damaged by fire. Consequently, the Winter Gardens were used as a temporary theatre. Although pretty from the outside, the venue was quite unsuitable for intimate performances. Without a proper theatre in town it didn't take long for some local businessmen to realise that here was a chance to initiate a bold new venture.

Frank Matcham

Chapter 2

Vestibules and Sloat Sliders
Cheltenham has a brand new theatre

By 1890 Cheltenham was without a theatre worthy of the name. It was clear that the town wanted a new theatre and two rival groups were established, each with their own proposals for the way forward. The Cheltenham Assembly Rooms and Theatre Company wanted to renovate and reconstruct their premises and provide not only a theatre but a concert hall and meeting rooms as well. The Cheltenham New Theatre and Opera House Company had plans to build a brand new, grand and prestigious theatre for the town.

The Assembly Rooms Theatre was to have a capacity of 1,420. The concert hall was to have a permanent stage at one end for the orchestra and the floor was to be restored so it would 'retain the excellent qualities it possesses for the purpose of the dance'.[1] The Company had engaged one of the leading theatre architects of the day, Frank Matcham, to provide them with ideas and plans.

However, it was the New Theatre and Opera House Company consortium, headed by a group of influential local businessmen, that won the race with their competitors eventually withdrawing their bid, realising that perhaps the town could not support two new theatres.

In September 1890 notice of a Subscription List for the Cheltenham Theatre and Opera House Co. Ltd. appeared in the *Cheltenham Chronicle*, showing a share capital of £6,000 in shares of £1 each. The Managing Director of the company was Colonel Agg, J. P. Other

The original façade of the theatre in 1891

directors of the new company were Lt. Colonel Croker-King, Colonel Smyth, Captain St. Clair-Ford J. P. and A. J. Skinner Esq. Mr. Charles Chappell was appointed acting manager for the theatre.[2]

Frank Matcham, clearly a pragmatist, promptly joined the victorious company. In the previous five or six years Matcham had already built or renovated fifteen theatres around the country. The Opera House, although a gem even by his standards, was a lot smaller than most of the theatres he was responsible for. In spite of its initial 1,500 capacity – well over twice as many as it currently holds – it was still dwarfed by most of its contemporaries.

Frank Matcham was born in the small town of Newton Abbot, Devon on 22nd November 1854. Christened Francis, he was one of nine children. Soon after his birth, the family moved to Torquay where his father took up a job as manager of the Mary Bridgeman Brewery and nearby Malt House.

The Bridgeman family seems to have taken young Frank under its wing. He was sent to Babbacombe School, one of the oldest and best in the area and, when he was fourteen, he was given a job in the office of architect George Sondon Bridgeman. Eager to get on, Matcham soon left Torquay and secured a job in London as an apprentice quantity surveyor. Upon qualifying, he returned to Bridgeman's as senior assistant during which time the company became pre-eminent in the region. It was at this time, in 1873, that Matcham worked on his first theatre project in Paignton.

Matcham's association with such a flourishing practice and influential family clearly stood him in good stead as he was to return to London in 1875 to work for the leading theatrical architects of the time, J. T. Robinson, in Mayfair.

Jethro Robinson was the most successful and knowledgeable theatre architects in the country and was consultant to the Lord Chamberlain. In 1892 he was described by Sir S. C. B. Ponsonby-Fane as 'a very clever designer of theatres who was not only aware of how theatres were built but how they worked'.

Matcham seems to have been a very ambitious young man who sought to use any opportunity to further his career. On 9th July 1877 he married the boss's youngest daughter, Hannah Maria Robinson, in St. James' Church on Pentonville Hill, just up the road from Kings Cross Station in London.

Even the choice of church seems to have been calculated, being the final resting place of the clown Joseph Grimaldi who had died in 1837.

A year later, Jethro Robinson died suddenly and the young Matcham promptly took over the practice, finishing the rebuilding of the Elephant and Castle Theatre which had been damaged by fire. A large proportion of Matcham's work was restoring and rebuilding theatres rather than creating them from scratch.

Fire was a great and permanent danger. The combination of highly combustible materials and gas lighting were to be responsible for the destruction of 137 important theatres between 1802 and 1896. Along with that went a significant loss of life due to lack of regulation and too few exits. As his career and experience developed, Matcham was to pioneer and incorporate many important safety features into the theatres he built.

Frank Matcham

In 1885, he completed the Royalty Theatre and Hengler's Grand Cirque, both in Glasgow and from then on his theatre work did not cease until 1913. He would sometimes work on as many as ten theatres in one year.

During his career Frank Matcham was to be responsible for building or restoring about two hundred theatres, including many of the most famous in the British Isles. In London he built the Coliseum, the Lyric Hammersmith, the Hippodrome and the Hackney Empire. Around the country he was responsible for the Grand, the Tower Circus and the Tower Ballroom in Blackpool, Her Majesty's in Aberdeen, the Theatre Royal in Newcastle and the Bristol Hippodrome. His most famous theatre is, without doubt, the London Palladium in Argyll Street near Oxford Circus.

It seems Matcham himself chose Regent Street in Cheltenham for the new theatre after considering several other sites. Although the plot was rather smaller than he would have liked, its location was ideal. The land backed on to the Plough Hotel on the High Street, which was the largest of the town's old coaching inns.

So handy was the hotel in fact, that artists appearing at the theatre would frequently send a boy across the yard with sixpence to bring back sustenance for them during a show. Sadly, the Plough was lost in the same Regent Arcade development that saw the back-stage area of the theatre rebuilt in the mid 1980s.

In contrast to the beautiful auditorium, the exterior of the New Theatre and Opera House was rather plain, in common with many theatres of the time. Just before the theatre's opening, *The Era* wrote that although the façade could not be described as imposing 'it is neat and in good taste. The red brick is relieved by stone pediments and sills to the doors and windows and upon the pediments there is, as a rule, some slight carving, heads in relief, representing Comedy, Tragedy etc.' *The Cheltenham Examiner* thought it 'quite good enough for the purpose'.

During the day the only sign of life would have been the box office which opened directly onto the street and had above it 'a carving of Shakespeare's head with allegorical design and background in low relief'. It was only in the evening with light flooding out through the windows and open doors and with carriages pulling up outside delivering the local gentry in all their finery that the theatre would begin to work its magic and the building would truly come alive.

There were originally three doorways, one for each area of the auditorium and, correspondingly, for each social class. Each entrance and lobby was physically separated to keep the classes apart. On the left hand corner, sheltered by a wrought iron and glass canopy, was the door that led into The Vestibule which was the entrance for Cheltenham's high society. This small, octagonal foyer of Moorish or Arabesque design had its own fireplace and champagne bar in the corner. According to *The Era* of 19th September 1891, 'Rich ornamentation has been lavished upon the ceiling which is elaborately gilded and painted, the prevailing colour being blue and this is intermingled with a sort of fawn, the whole being picked out with Indian reds'. *The Cheltenham Examiner* on 23rd September 1891 reported what happened when you entered the auditorium:

'From the Vestibule, a broad corridor conducts the visitor into the Orchestra Stalls and from the same point, a stone staircase, seven feet wide, is carried up to a large landing, on one side of which is a crush room, with swing doors opening onto the Dress Circle promenade, the staircase is continued up to a corridor running round the back of the Upper Circle, also entered by swing doors.

'An elegantly fitted refreshment saloon is approached off the second landing of the staircase. This saloon, like The Vestibule, is an octagon in form, is lighted by a graceful electrolier, and has a prettily-embellished ceiling'.

left: The Vestibule, lobby for the Dress Circle

above: Advert by the original seat manufacturers

below: Jonas Binns of Halifax

From the street, the centre doors led down some steps straight through into the Pit while the right hand doors led up the long, turning stone stairs to the Gallery or 'gods'.

The comfort of the patrons was also determined by where they sat. The Dress Circle had fine, upholstered, armchair-like seats. The rest consisted of benches; upholstered in the Upper Circle, not upholstered in the Pit and plain wooden benches in the Gallery. These cramped seating arrangements meant it was possible to get more than twice as many people into the auditorium compared to today.

The centrepiece of the auditorium was the chandelier-like, so-called Sun Burner. While it provided lighting for the auditorium by gas, estimated at a respectable 500 candle-power, its main function was as a ventilator, drawing up all the stale air and evacuating it through the roof.

The Sun Burner hung from the centre of the beautiful domed ceiling decorated by Jonas Binns & Co. of Halifax. It was described by *The Era* as follows:

'The ceiling has been treated with great skill, and looks very handsome. In the dome, the panels are painted in sky blue, with birds flying about. There are four panels in the ceiling, filled in with paintings, which typify the four elements – earth, air, fire, and water. In the 'outer ring' of the ceiling there are eight panels, containing paintings of cherubs,

Chapter 2 Vestibules and Sloat Sliders

or 'cupids' according to the popular description, symbolical of music, painting, poetry, writing, the arts etc. Over the private boxes, there are medallions hand-painted with trophies of musical instruments. In the corners of what is now commonly called the proscenium, there are figure paintings on a gold ground, representing Comedy and Tragedy.'[3]

The top corners of the proscenium arch were also embellished with fine, figurative paintings. Again these were painted on canvas, probably in the Binns' workshop in Yorkshire, and finished and retouched once they were in place in the theatre. The original proscenium arch was a *faux* marble known as *scagliola*. Original invoices for the building of the theatre describe this as being like Castille, an Italian marble usually cream in colour. The craftsmen who undertook this highly skilled work were Bellman & Ivey of London, leading exponents of *scagliola* in the country. The sections were created off-site and brought from London to be fixed in place.

The main colour scheme for the auditorium consisted mostly of blue, gold and cream. The *Cheltenham Examiner* was actually surprised by how good it looked. 'We must frankly confess that even a sanguine expectation of the beauty and size is exceeded by results.'[4] A special blue and gold talc paper was selected for the walls.

Pursuing Matcham's concern for public safety, each area of the auditorium was designated more than one exit point and all eleven exterior doors opened outwards and were fitted with the new Kay's Safety Bolt, or crash bar, as they are known. The Opera House was one of the first public buildings in the country to be fitted with these locks. The long stone staircase leading down from the gallery was fitted with patent Doulton non-slip treads. It was estimated that a full house of 1,500 people could be safely evacuated from the theatre in three or four minutes.

A fragment of wallpaper believed to have been from the original decor

The backstage area, or stage-house, was typical of the theatres of the time being made nearly entirely of wood. It had a full suite of sub-stage machinery based on the traditions of the *English Wood Stage*. Although most of the stage-house remained in its original state right up until 1983, all of the sub-stage machinery probably disappeared in 1929 when the stage was considered unsafe and rebuilt. Anything that survived would have been lost in 1948[5] when another new stage was installed. However, tell-tale marks on the walls did remain.

In 1983 Spencer Mort of Cirencester inspected the Everyman just before the bulldozers moved in to demolish the stage-house. He found indications that the stage had been divided into nine 9½ inch wide sliding sections called 'Sloat Sliders' with two three-foot bridges and one eighteen-inch bridge interspaced. This arrangement would seem to be very similar to that of the Leicester Theatre Royal of 1873. The narrow 'Sloat Cuts' would have been used for raising scenery, ground rows and such like and the wider bridges for set pieces and actors. There would also have been a grave trap-door centre downstage. One original feature that did remain in the theatre was the enormous wooden wheel in the grid that was used for winding the paint frame up and down.

Originally there were five dressing rooms which were up the stone stairs just inside the stage door. These rooms later became offices when a new extension was built on stage left of the stage house to accommodate workshops and the new dressing rooms above.

Shortly before its opening, *The Cheltenham Examiner* was very impressed with the theatre though, it had some reservations about its location. '… the Cheltenham New Theatre and Opera House is one of the very best buildings in of the kind in England – one of the most elegant, one of the most convenient and one of the safest. As to whether or not the ideal site had been chosen, some slight difference of opinion may exist … the site in Regent Street, immediately close as it is to the High-street and the Promenade, is doubtless as good as any that could be found.'[6]

Frank Matcham died of blood poisoning on 17th May 1920 at his home in Southend-on-Sea and is buried in Highgate Cemetery in London. Only about twenty-five of his theatres survive more or less intact, with the gutted shells of another dozen or so continuing as bingo halls, cinemas or night clubs.

His obituary in *The Times* on 20th May paid tribute by saying, 'Although his buildings were often excellent in external design, his chief concern was with the interior construction, his object being always that of enabling every member of the audience to obtain a good view of the stage. In this he was remarkably successful'.

This was certainly true of the Everyman, which is now the oldest surviving Matcham auditorium still in constant use. Of all the theatres Matcham built, Cheltenham was also the second smallest with the pretty Theatre Royal in Wakefield, Yorkshire being the smallest.

Lillie Langtry

Chapter 3

Jersey Lily and Lillah on a chair
The best show in town as the new theatre opens

The thrill and excitement that surrounded the opening of Frank Matcham's New Theatre and Opera House on the evening of Thursday, 1st October 1891 was almost tangible. Crowds in Regent Street jostled to catch a glimpse of the cream of Cheltenham society as the horse-drawn carriages drew up outside the brilliantly illuminated new building. They had also come to catch a glimpse of a famous lady who, if not Royalty herself, was someone who had been very close to it in the portly shape of the future King Edward VII.

'At enormous expense,' Lillie Langtry, along with her 'powerful' Princess Theatre Company from London, had been engaged to present the opening production, 'An original drama in four acts' by Tom Taylor entitled *Lady Clancarty* or *Wedded and Wooed*.

The choice of Mrs. Langtry was inspired. She was probably the most famous woman of her day, what we would call a celebrity, although it would probably be more accurate to describe her as a courtesan. It seemed her career as an actress was merely cashing in on her existing fame and while the public flocked to see her, the critics were rarely complementary. Her secret was that she had friends in high places. 'I resent Mrs. Langtry,' said George Bernard Shaw, 'she has no right to be intelligent, daring and independent as well as lovely. It is a frightening combination of attributes.'[1]

But it wasn't just Mrs. Langtry that thrilled the crowds. The building itself was the co-star that evening. *The Cheltenham Examiner* waxed

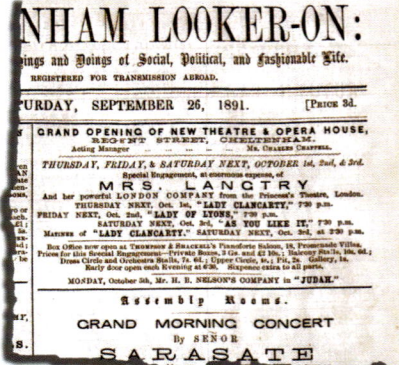

Miss Lillah McCarthy

lyrical about the auditorium, 'And now, the majority of the audience seated, and the multitudinous lamps casting their brilliant rays on the delicate Louis XV decorations of tier-fronts and boxes, and the gay draperies of the fashionable fair, the tableau curtain, of sumptuous amber plush, is drawn aside, disclosing an Act drop, which though perhaps scarcely pictorial enough to please some tastes, is yet exceedingly effective. It represents a painted fan, having for its subject a group of ladies and gallants in early Georgian costume, who are indulging in a minuet in a garden of unimpeachable verdure, under a sky of Italian blue'.[2]

The Era, having followed the theatre's development in great detail for several weeks, was complementary about the final result. 'The new and elegant temple of the drama was opened on Thursday evening, with an amount of éclat that augurs well for its prosperity.'[3]

The *Cheltenham Looker-On* was particularly impressed with the lighting which illuminated not only the tasteful décor of the auditorium but 'the gay throng' within it.

Seats for the opening night were not cheap. Boxes cost either £3 or £2.10s (£2.50) and a seat in the Dress Circle cost 7/6 (37½p). Bearing in mind that in those days a teacher would have only earned £2.60 a week, one can appreciate how exclusive the event sought to be. Due to the high prices for the gala opening night, the performance was not sold out, although the houses for the first and three subsequent nights were described by *The Cheltenham Examiner* as 'satisfactory and encouraging.'

One member of the audience on that first night was a fifteen-year-old girl called Lillah McCarthy. The previous evening Lillah, already a seasoned local performer, had been brought into the theatre and placed on a chair to test the auditorium's acoustics. She had been born in Cheltenham in 1875 next to the Plough Hotel where her father was manager.

The building, now a Burger King, is part of the complex in which the Everyman now stands. Lillah made her first public appearance fifty yards away at the Assembly Rooms on 8th April 1881. On another occasion she was later taken to meet Frank Benson when his company played the Opera House, and after hearing her recite, he told her father he should send her to London to be trained as an actress.[4]

George Bernard Shaw was to take an interest in Lillah's career as well. After seeing her perform he wrote, 'It is an actress's profession to be extraordinary but Lillah was extraordinary even among actresses'.[5] In 1900 Lillah appeared for the first time at the Opera House in *Man and His Makers*, *The Silver King* and *The Sign of the Cross* with the Wilson Barrett Company. She returned three years later, this time with her brother Daniel in the company.

In 1905 Shaw asked Miss McCarthy to create the role of Ann Whitefield in his new play *Man and Superman*. This was to be the start of a long association with the Irish playwright and she went on to create five more of his heroines. Lillah married one of the great actor-managers of the day, Harley Granville Barker, and became one of the most celebrated actresses of the time. She died in London in April 1960.

Lillah's day was still a way off and that mild October evening belonged exclusively to Mrs. Langtry. Lillie Langtry had been born Emilie Charlotte Le Breton on 13th October 1853 on the island of Jersey. She was the daughter of the Dean of Jersey who had gained rather a reputation as a philanderer.[6] In 1874 Lillie married wealthy Irish landowner Edward Langtry, the brother-in-law of her brother William's wife. They left the Channel Islands, eventually settling in rented accommodation in London's Belgravia.

A couple of years later her beauty opened the doors of London society and she soon became involved with some of the great artists of Victorian London, including the Pre-Raphaelites Sir John Everett Millais and Sir Edward Burne-Jones, both of whom immortalised the *Jersey Lily* in their work. It was not long before she met the future king, Prince Albert Edward, in 1877.

He became infatuated with Langtry and she became his semi-official mistress. She was even presented to Edward's mother, Queen Victoria. The affair lasted three years and made her the talk of the town. However, she was dropped by the Prince after misbehaving at a dinner party, although her star had already been eclipsed by the arrival in London of Sarah Bernhardt in June 1879.

In 1881, at the suggestion of Oscar Wilde, Lillie Langtry took up acting causing a scandal by being the first society lady to take up a profession that was regarded as little more than prostitution. Although she would continue acting, her affair the following year with American millionaire Frederic Gebhard led to the only true love of her life, horse racing.

As the audience settled down in Cheltenham's New Theatre and Opera House for the first night performance of *Lady Clancarty*, the

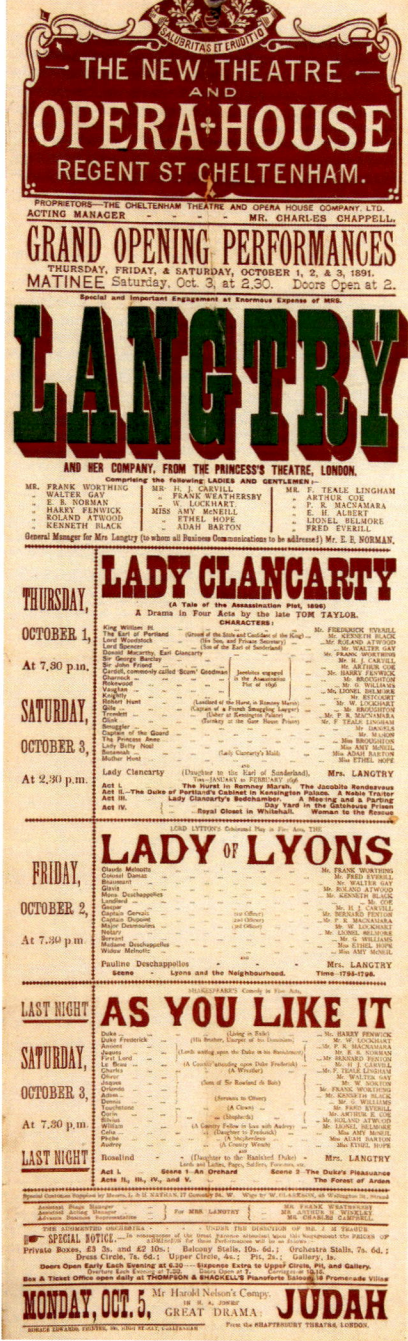

The Opera House at the turn of the century

twenty-two piece orchestra, under the direction of Mr. J. M. Teague, struck up the National Anthem 'which announced the commencement of the performance and formed the signal for the audience to rise *en masse*'.

When the curtain finally rose, Lillie Langtry delivered an address, before the play started, to commemorate the occasion …

Hail Sylvan city, for thy vanishing stage
With us returns at last a golden age
'Tis strange that Thespis hence so long should roam
Where could he find a more congenial home
Than this fair valley of eternal hills
Where shrines of Faith and Learning greet the eye
Nor fog nor factory smoke pollute the sky …

At the end of the second act, halfway through the play, the cry went up for Frank Matcham, Charles Chappell, the acting manager, and Mr. Butler who represented the building contractor. When Matcham appeared before the curtain the applause with which he was greeted plainly indicated that his efforts had thoroughly satisfied the Cheltenham theatre-going public.

Mr. Charles Chappell then spoke, thanking the audience for the kind manner in which they had shown their appreciation of his services. He told them that for the forthcoming season he had booked some of the best companies of the day. He went on to say that he had received many telegrams of congratulation, notably from Mr. D'Oyly Carte.

A couple of days later the *Cheltenham Looker-On* described the grand opening at length:

'The special event of the week now drawing to a close has been the opening of the new theatre which took place last Thursday, with no more ceremony than the recital of a prologue which contained local and personal allusions usually met within such poetic flights, but if Aldermanic robes shed no sombre brightness on the scene, the cloaks of another kind and hue which had been for many days before so prominent a feature in certain windows in the promenade, added to the general brightness produced in part by the tasteful decoration of the building, and in part by the gay throng which filled it to overflowing. As the electric light burst forth in the hitherto dimly lit building and disclosed its full ensemble, the applause of the audience bespoke their admiration of the handsome edifice, and the cheers were renewed as the National Anthem, finely played by the augmented orchestra under Mr. J. M. Teague commenced the evening's proceedings.

'The entrance of Mrs. Langtry to recite the prologue was the signal for another outburst, and on her retirement, the happy recipient of a handsome bouquet, the audience resigned itself to the performance of the night. Of this, on such an occasion, criticism may fairly take the form of praise, Mrs. Langtry's acting in the part of Lady Clancarty answering all reasonable expectations, while Mr. Frank Worthington as Lord Clancarty, Mr. Everill as King William III, Mr. Fenwick and Miss Amy McNeil displayed considerable power.'[7]

Matcham, speaking at an after-show supper held at the Plough, said that he was much obliged for their kind appreciation and in particular for the complimentary references by the host. He claimed he had only been doing his duty and done no more than a builder, upholsterer or bricklayer.

On the Friday night, 2nd October, Langtry's company performed Lord Lytton's *The Lady of Lyons*. For the Saturday matinee, *Lady Clancarty* was reprised followed, in the evening, by a presentation of Shakespeare's *As You Like It* with Mrs. Langtry playing Rosalind, one of her most celebrated roles.

Although for the citizens of Cheltenham, its dignitaries and those involved with the new theatre 1st October 1891 would have been a very important day, for Mrs. Langtry the three-day engagement was almost certainly just another job. But it was, in all probability, one that would have been a little inconvenient because, given the state of her personal life, she certainly had other things on her mind.

In October 1891 Lillie was in the final throes of a tempestuous relationship that had started in April that year with George Alexander Baird, a millionaire amateur jockey and pugilist. He was an obsessively jealous and brutal man, who beat her frequently, but would pay her '£5,000 remorse money' afterwards. In this way she came to own a fine chestnut colt named *Milford*, who was to go on and win many races.

In the autumn of 1891, soon after her visit to Cheltenham, Lillie's company was on tour in the north. Baird, known as 'The Squire', went to Scotland, ostensibly for the racing at Ayr, but in fact to keep an eye on his mistress. When Lillie had finished her tour, she returned to

George Alexander Baird

Lillie Langtry

London while Baird remained for the shooting. Almost immediately upon her return she met up with one of her admirers, Robert Peel who persuaded her to go off to Paris with him. She, of course, readily agreed, seeing the chance to shop in the Paris fashion houses at his expense.

When Baird got back to London and found that Lillie had gone off with another man, he immediately went in pursuit. Finding her in her Paris hotel room he beat her so severely that she ended up in hospital for two weeks, covered in bruises, nursing two black eyes and a swollen nose. He also tore all her clothing to shreds and wrecked the hotel room.

A warrant for the arrest of Baird was issued by the French police but, as it happened, he was already in the cells following another fracas at the brothel to which he had gone after the assault at the hotel. Lillie Langtry died in Monte Carlo on February 12th 1929, aged 75, and was buried at St. Saviour's Church on Jersey.

The first year of the new theatre progressed with the presentation of a new show every week by a different touring company. Immediately following Lillie Langtry's three day visit, Mr. Harold B. Nelson's company came in on 5th October with *Judah* which *The Cheltenham Looker-On* announced was 'a remarkable play that claims with justice to be one of the finest productions in recent times'.

William Swift was now head-master of Churchdown School near Gloucester, about eight miles from Cheltenham. He was still a keen theatre-goer and still meticulously kept his diary. He recorded a visit to the new Opera House with his son, exactly a year after it had opened.

On 8th October 1892 they rode into town and left their tricycles in Bayshill Inn yard and walked across the Promenade to Regent Street. Swift thought the decoration of the new theatre very beautiful, particularly the fine ceiling. He also admired the electric lighting and the gold and brown colour scheme. He wrote that he had paid 1/6 (7½p) for a seat in the Pit and had a drink in the 'subterranean refreshment bar' which was situated under the foyer.[7] He did not record any of the rowdyism he had encountered in the final days of the Old Royal Well Theatre.

A couple of celebrations took place around the first anniversary of the new theatre. The annual demonstration and entertainment in connection with the Conservative Club took place in the theatre in front of 'an immense audience'. Selections from *Macbeth*, a musical entertainment and the farcical comedy of *Turned Up* were presented. A most noteworthy feature of the show was the really powerful performance of Lady Macbeth by sixteen-year-old Miss McCarthy while Mr. Braine gave a creditable rendering of Macbeth. Miss Lena Young was specially retained to support the amateurs in the comedy, the principal parts in which were played by Messrs Wells, Chappell and Packmen.

The first annual supper given for the employees of the Opera House was held at the Plough Hotel on the evening of Friday, 11th November 1892 with Mr. Chappell, who was still only the acting-manager, presiding. During the evening, Mr. Wilson, the principal stage-carpenter, presented Mr. Chappell with a silver-mounted ebony walking stick, a morocco cigar-case and silver match-box, subscribed for as a mark of respect by the employees. Mr. Chappell, in acknowledging the gift, expressed his gratification at the good feeling which existed in the theatre and was pleased to say that his staff had given the greatest satisfaction to the managers of all the companies who had visited the theatre.[9]

A fragment of one of the paintings which decorated the original proscenium arch
Photo: Michael Hasted

May 4th 1900. With Aunt Alice & Charley —

Opera House
CHELTENHAM.

PROPRIETORS:—
THE CHELTENHAM THEATRE & OPERA HOUSE Co. Ltd.

Acting Manager:—
Mr GEORGE ABEL.

MANAGING DIRECTORS
Chairman:— Lt. COLONEL C. E. CROKER-KING, J.P.
COL. AGG, J.P. COL. ROGERS, J.P. Mr A. J. SHINNER.

SALUBRITAS ET ERUDITIO

Telephone No 92
Box Office open from 10 to 5 at Dale, Forty & Co, The Promenade.

Horace Edwards, Cheltenham.

Chapter 4

The future looks bright
The early years 1900-1918

Charles Chappell, who had been the General Manager of the Opera House since its opening, died in February 1899 and was replaced for a short time by George Abel. His place was taken in 1900 by Mr. H. Oswald Redford who was to remain in the job until his death in 1924.

By this time The Opera House had established a regular pattern of weekly shows. The D'Oyly Carte Company with Gilbert and Sullivan operas was a regular visitor and there were lots of touring plays and a pantomime at Christmas. There were many other shows described as 'burlesque operas.'

Cheltenham at the turn of the century was still quite a lively place and The Opera House was not the only source of entertainment in town. In October 1900, a Catherine Wilson, who advertised herself as 'Madame de Mundella, the lady palmist from the Royal Aquarium', was sentenced to one month's imprisonment with hard labour for fortune telling. Evidence was produced to show that since her arrival in Cheltenham on 4th October, the accused had carried on a prosperous business. Among her clients was a policeman in plain clothes for whom she predicted a successful career as a solicitor's clerk. It was stated that one girl who had been summoned as a witness was too ill to give evidence in consequence of what she had been told by the accused.[1]

MR. H. OSWALD REDFORD.

This Song must not be Sung in Theatres and Music Halls without the permission of Mr. Arthur Lloyd.

And That's Why I've Not Got 'Em On.

Written, Composed and Sung By

Arthur Lloyd.

Copyright.

LONDON.
HOPWOOD & CREW, 42, NEW BOND STREET, W.

Price 4/-

Arthur Lloyd was one of the turn of the century's most successful and famous music hall artists and song writers. He appeared at the Opera House, Cheltenham in March 1902 with his two daughters. One review for their sketch, *Little Charlie* or *The Twin Sisters*, said, 'It is well acted and last night the large house showed its appreciation by hearty applause'.[2]

Other theatres in Cheltenham at this time included the Pavilion in Montpellier Gardens, but this was little more than a bandstand for pierrot, end-of-pier variety or children's entertainment in the summer. The Assembly Rooms were still functioning, as was the Corn Exchange. The Winter Gardens were still going strong and, soon after the turn of the century, began providing some real, new-fangled competition for the Opera House.

opposite: Sheet music of an Arthur Lloyd song
Courtesy of Peter Charlton and www.arthurlloyd.co.uk

above: The Hippodrome Theatre in Albion Street, later to become the Coliseum.
Courtesy of Roger Beacham

Chapter 4 The future looks bright

above: The *Robinson Crusoe* company, 1912 with H. Oswald Redford centre, second row

opposite: The theatre undergoing its first major refurbishment in 1913

The first moving pictures were shown in Imperial Square as early as 1903 when there was a performance of animated images of the *Great Delhi Durbar*.

The Assembly Rooms and other venues had put on similar performances even earlier, but it was the arrival of the first genuine movies that really caused a stir. The Winter Gardens' New Kinema opened in 1912 and showed films up until the outbreak of war in 1939.

The Assembly Rooms, The Opera House's main competition, were demolished in 1900 and, until the Town Hall was built in 1902-3 alongside the Winter Gardens, the theatre had things very much its own way. However, in 1913 the theatre-goers of Cheltenham were presented with a serious alternative to the Opera House.

On the August Bank Holiday 1913, a brand new theatre, The Hippodrome, was opened in Albion Street by Cecil Gill Smith. *The Stage* reported, 'The new building is being erected on a corner site for Messrs. Gillsmith Ltd. The architect is Mr. Herbert T. Rainger of Cheltenham.

'Seating accommodation will be provided for close upon a thousand people, and in addition to this, there will be a spacious lounge, with full view of the stage, at the back of the circle, where afternoon teas will be served. The entrance foyer will be decorated in Tudor style in dark oak, and special attention is being given to the decoration of the auditorium. A novel colour scheme of copper flame rouge and French grey should give a delightfully restful, yet smart and effective result. Indirect lighting is being adopted throughout the auditorium'.[3] The Coliseum was finally demolished in June 2011.

It was probably the perceived competition in Albion Street that prompted the first major redecoration of the Opera House in July 1913. After 22 years, the theatre was in need of some refurbishment. The auditorium was completely repainted and all the seats, upholstery and carpets were replaced.

In the 1960s and seventies there were still a few people around who could remember the very early days of the Opera House. In 1963, the then General Manager of the Everyman, John Ridley, received a letter from an elderly gentleman in Toronto signing himself merely as 'An old Cheltonian.' He wrote, '... now I can remember that theatre being opened, that's a long time ago, the Manager's name I think was Mr. Redfern [sic] and a smart man too at that. There was some good plays there then, like *Charley's Aunt*, *The Merry Widow*, *Geisha* and *The Bell of New York* all these come right off London and, of course, there was all the operas too, first class ones.

THE CHELTENHAM CHRONICLE AND Glo'shire Graphic

ART AND LITERARY SUPPLEMENT

No. 837. Saturday, January 13, 1917. [Circulation Guaranteed over 12,000 copies weekly.]

8th Gloucestershire Regiment

WHAT WAS LEFT OF THEM.

Surviving officers, warrant officers, and senior N.C.O.'s of the original 8th Battalion Gloucestershire Regiment.
Top row.—C.-Q.-M.-S. Minchin, C.-S.-M. Perry, C.-S.-M. C. Johnson, C.-S.-M. A. Johnson, C.-Q.-M.-S. Dale.
Middle row.—Sergt. Walden, Sergt. Sparks, C.-Q.-M.-S. Farnham, Sergt. Sheppard, C.-Q.-M.-S. Weaver.
Sitting.—Act. R.-Q.-M.-S. Fowles, Act. Q.-M. Evans, Sec.-Lieut. Wookey, Major C. H. Harding, R.-S.-M. Vaughan, C.-S.-M. Jones, C.-S.-M. Bishop.
These are practically all North Gloucestershire men (from Cheltenham, Stroud, Cirencester, Gloucester, and Tewkesbury).

THEATRE & OPERA HOUSE, CHELTENHAM.
TO-DAY AT TWO AND SEVEN O'CLOCK.
LAST TWO PERFORMANCES OF
"Jack and the Beanstalk."
NEXT WEEK:
"POTASH AND PERLMUTTER IN SOCIETY."
Six Nights, 7.30; Matinee Saturday, 2.30.

PALACE PICTURE PLAYHOUSE,
HIGH STREET, CHELTENHAM.
Monday, Tuesday, and Wednesday:
"THE COWARD."
A Beautifully-produced Patriotic 5-Act Drama.
Times of Showing: 3, 6.15, and 8.30 Daily.
"DASH AND COURAGE."
A 2-Reel Triangle-Keystone Comedy.
Thursday, Friday, and Saturday:
"SECOND THOUGHTS."
The Story of a Girl's Temptation and Triumph.
Times of Showing: 3, 6.15, and 8.30 Daily.
"HER PAINTED HERO."
A 2-Act Keystone Comedy of Stage Life.

Old Selected SCOTCH WHISKIES.
B BLEND 25/6 per Gall.; 4/3 per Bott.
BB BLEND 27/- per Gall.; 4/6 per Bott.
BBB BLEND 28/6 per Gall.; 4/9 per Bott.

BARTHOLOMEW,
419-420 HIGH ST., CHELTENHAM.

TAWNY PORTS. Old in Wood.
30/-, 36/-, 42/- per Bott.;
2/6, 3/-, 3/6 per Bott. Tel. 135

MARTIN AND CO., LTD.,
Promenade, Cheltenham,
Purchase for Cash ANTIQUES of all kinds, including OLD SILVER, JEWELLERY, SHEFFIELD PLATE, CHINA, COINS, MINIATURES, &c.
High Prices Given for Rare Pieces.

SLADE'S SHOE SALE
TO-DAY, and Until January 31.
INCREASING SCARCITY OF LEATHER WILL MAKE BOOTS AND SHOES EXTREMELY EXPENSIVE AND DIFFICULT TO OBTAIN. EVERY PAIR AT SALE PRICE IS AN EXCELLENT INVESTMENT.
Imperial House, Promenade, Cheltenham.

Corset Sale.
GREAT BARGAINS
In all Sizes, from 5s. 6d.

ANNETTE,
Corset Maker,
28 CLARENCE STREET, Cheltenham.

For the Best **PIANOS, DALE, FORTY and Co., Ltd**

'Yes Sir, I can remember seeing The Cabs and Flys (no motors then) lined up from the Star right down to Smiths Livery Stables, that was when the operas was on; then there was big Charley dressed in uniform in the Vestibule calling out for the Big Shots for their Cabs to go home.

'The two scene shifters were Bart Wilson and Bill Radway, Bill's mother and sister was the costume women for the actresses. Shakespeare Shenton was the bill poster. At half time you could get a pass out and go over to the Star or Dobells pub and get a pint for 3d. or half pint for a penny ha'penny.

'Yes sir, Cheltenham was a quiet place then, no factories was allowed there, at 11.30 at night High Street and Promenade was as quiet as a morgue, not now I'll bet! Please excuse this writing as I am over 90, I should like once more to see the Old Town where I was born on the Swindon Road. I get the *Chronicle* sent out to me.'

Malcolm Farquhar, who was Director of Productions in the 1970s and eighties, remembers meeting someone who recalled the very early days of the theatre as well, 'When I was director in Cheltenham there was a little old lady who lived in Charlton Kings, used to lend us a lot of furniture for plays.

She told me once how, as a little girl – that must have been in the 1890s – she used to be brought to the theatre with her father in a brougham, a small horse drawn carriage. She had a silver cushion to sit on in the stalls so she could see. She remembers her father used to drink champagne in the interval from the little bar in the corner of foyer.'

In 1915 the first change of management occurred at the Opera House when the theatre was leased to Mr. Robert Redford. Mr. Redford appointed his brother, the incumbent manager H. Oswald Redford, to run the theatre on his behalf.

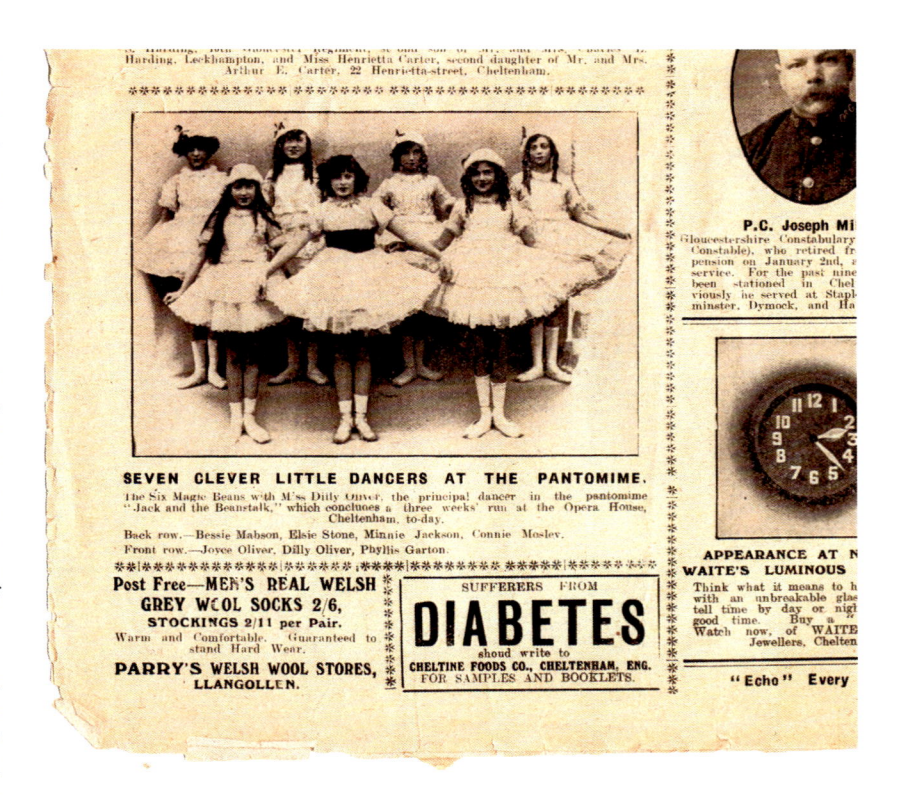

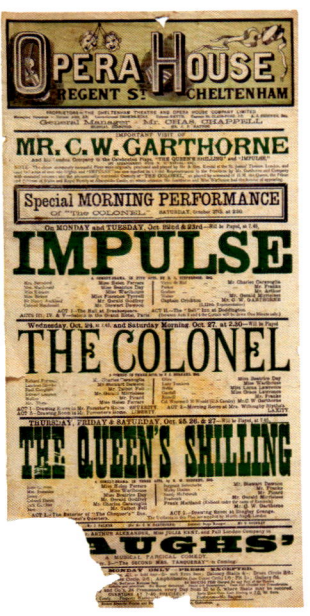

THE Looker-On

A Social, Political and Fashionable Review for Ch...

Year, No. 4266.   SATURDAY, JANUARY 12, 1918

The Winter Gardens from Queens Hotel, Che...

& Opera House
Robert Redford.
Manager H. Oswald Redford
...Y at 2 & 7 p.m.
"...N DAYS' LEAVE."

...k. Next Week,
...14th, and
...s at 7 30.

WINTER GARDEN PICTURE H...
Special Attractions for Week commencing ...
MONDAY, TUESDAY AND WEDNESDAY
MARY PICK...

"A CHINESE HONEYMOON"
"Play Pictorial Series 18"

Wilds.

The Opera House, Cheltenham
TEL. 5144 & 5145 (2 lines)

Dress Circle
Second House

...DEC 1939
...including Tax
SEAT No.
14

This Ticket cannot be exchanged or money refunded

THE OPERA HOUSE
TELEPHONE ... 5144 and 5145 (Two Lines)
Director ... WILFRED SIMPSON

Phone 2819
PROMENADE CAFÉ
Real Garden Oiled with VITA Glass
GLOUCESTERSHIRE DAIRY CO.

H. M. TENNENT, LTD.
presents
"REBECCA"
by DAPHNE DU MAURIER

WEEK
7-0 NIGHTLY 7-0
MATINEE SATURDAY ONLY at 2-30

WELCOME RETURN VISIT
OF
Olive Fox & Clarkson Rose
— IN —
TWINKLE
...DIE CHILDS   WITH   RUPERT RO...
AUDREY

Chapter 5

A mauve dress and the Northwest Frontier
The theatre between the wars

Ruby Mitton (nee Midwinter) has memories of the theatre going back to the 1920s when she appeared there as a child. She recalls, 'A touring company brought *A Midsummer Night's Dream* to the Opera House. They needed fairies so they asked local dance schools to provide some children. I attended a dancing school run by a Miss Lapham, on the Promenade, and was chosen to participate. It was about 1923 so I would have been about four years old. I was given a mauve dress to wear which they produced out of a big hamper. The costume was much too long for me and I was most upset that they just tied it up with string round my waist. Of course I didn't realise that it wouldn't be seen from the front. Another thing I remember was the donkey head worn by Bottom. That really frightened me'.

The years after the First World War were, for the Opera House, very successful commercially and, more significantly, the theatre had become an important cultural and social centre for the town.

Ronald Blower's mother, Hilda Niblett, used to work in the theatre as an usherette in the mid 1920s. It was through the Opera House that she met Ronald's father. 'My father was in the army in India, on the Northwest Frontier, and all the soldiers there were keen to have female pen-friends back home. There was a group of them from Cheltenham and they got in touch with the usherettes who worked in the theatre. So, all the girls put their names in a hat and all the soldiers' names were put in another and the bits of paper were pulled out, one by one and paired up. My mother got George Blower, my father, and her best friend got Bob who was my father's best friend. They started writing to each other and when the boys came back to Cheltenham, they all got married. My maternal grandmother used to run the old fire brigade when it was a private company with its fire station in St. James' Square.'

St. James' Square was, at the time, the location of one of Cheltenham's three main railway station, aptly called the St. James' Station. It played quite an important role in the running of the Opera House as Bryan Mabbett remembers.

'I was ten in 1936 and my dad, Robert Mabbett, sometimes used to take me into the theatre with him where he worked most evenings in the flies. During the day he was a van driver for Shirers & Lances, the old department store in the Promenade, and his mate, Mr. Reichelt, worked there too.

'As well as pulling the ropes in the flies, one of my dad's other duties was to take the scenery from the show that had just finished on a Saturday night to the railway station so it could go off to its next venue. He would then wait around and bring back the sets and props for the new one when they arrived on a later train. Everything used to go by train in those days. My dad would carry all the stuff in a horse-drawn wagon; there wasn't a lorry or anything. The horse and cart belonged to a Mr. Marks who lived down the Lower High Street by the gas works where Tesco's now stands. He used to loan it to my dad and I often went with him to the old St. James' Station by St. Gregory's church. When they'd finished for the night my dad would take the horse to the stables that used to be behind the old Royal Hotel in the High Street, where the Beechwood Arcade now stands. A lot of the performers from the theatre used to stay there I remember.'

Cheltenham was not short of places of entertainment between the wars. The New Pavilion in Montpellier Gardens, which was managed by Alfred W. Newton, was still going strong with Summer Season and there were several cinemas in town.

The only full time professional theatre in Cheltenham in 1925, apart from the Opera House, was the former Gillsmith's Hippodrome. The theatre had been bought from Gillsmith in 1920 by Mr. H. G. Beard of Gloucester along with a cinema in North Street, approximately where the Job Centre now stands. The Hippodrome was renamed The Coliseum and continued to present music hall and variety.

Beard had ambitions to put on dramas and musical comedies but the conditions of his licence prevented him from doing so. In April 1921, he applied for a new license which would enable him to compete with

Queues along Regent Street for
No, No, Nanette, April 1927
Courtesy of Jill Waller

the Opera House by mounting touring plays and musicals. The license was granted. The Coliseum was now in direct competition with the theatre in Regent Street.[1]

In 1925 the Opera House was sold to a new company and the shareholders received £1.11s.6d (£1.57) for their £1 shares. Shareholders of the new company included Mr. Arthur Cole, Mr. John Holborow and Mr. Wilfred Simpson who was appointed Manager – a position he held until 1955.

The first thing the new owners did was to completely renovate the theatre at an estimated cost of between £5,000 and £6,000. *The Echo* reported that, 'Simplicity and good taste may be said to be the keynote of the scheme of re-decoration. Gone are the big yellow parrots saying nasty things to big grey pigeons on an impossible tangle of vine branches that used to aggravate us every time we saw them; and in the place of the gaudy wallpaper on which they appeared is a simple treatment of electric blue, the latter forms a perfect background to the cream and gold of the balcony fronts, the pillars, and the ornamental details in general. The excellent paintings in the ceiling and the spandrels are, of course, retained'.[2]

THE OPERA HOUSE

TELEPHONE ... ... 5144 (Two Lines)
Managing Director.................................WILFRED SIMPSON

PROGRAMME

"SKYLARK"

WITH

JOHN CLEMENTS
CONSTANCE CUMMINGS
VALERIE TAYLOR
JACK MELFORD

Commencing Monday, February 9th

7-0 - ONCE NIGHTLY - 7-0

Matinees — Thursday and Saturday at 2-30 p.m.

1927 saw the establishment of a partnership and relationship that would extend right until the very last days of the Opera House. Reg Maddox, who took over the Theatre Royal Bath in 1938, was invited by Wilfred Simpson to stage a pantomime at Cheltenham. The arrangement was to continue for several years and Frank Maddox, Reg's son, was the Managing Director of the Opera House when it closed in 1959.

In 1929 the theatre was to undergo probably the biggest change in its history. The Cheltenham Theatre & Opera House Company sold the building to a concern called Cinema House Ltd. who intended turning the Opera House into a cinema now that the talkies had arrived. The managing director of the new Cinema House company was Eric V. Hakim, but Wilfred Simpson was asked to stay on as General Manager. The cinema license granted by the Council stipulated that stage shows should continue to be presented at the theatre, although it was the film shows that dominated.

Clearly a cinema has different requirements to a theatre and the *Echo* was invited in to have a look around. 'The first of the many additions our representative noticed on entering the theatre was the large white screen across the stage for the pictures. It is stretched on a framework of nearly a ton weight, but a mere touch on a pulley lifts it away to the 'flies,' leaving the stage clear. The screen is to be artistically set in black and there will be a handsome gold stage curtain automatically controlled.

'A glance at the rear of the stage reveals a new feature, for there are placed the two towers, eighteen feet high, in which are mounted the mighty loud speakers, with an aperture of 5ft x 4ft. through which the talking part of the talking picture business is done. Their horns are 16 feet long, and at the base end are but an inch in diameter, although they expand to the huge aperture mentioned'.[3]

In addition to the new equipment, a lot of refurbishment was undertaken. Two hundred and fifty tip-up seats in blue plush were installed in the Upper Circle and Gallery, and new house lights were put in which enabled the auditorium to 'be lighted on the new system of dimmers, by the use of which the light from the electric lamps can be raised or lowered to any desired degree instead of flashed on and off'. Illuminated signs in the auditorium were also put in place and the front of the building was lit up with flood lights.[4] The entire change over to cinema was said to have 'cost anything up to £15,000' according to the *Echo*.

The new cinema evidently considered itself as a cut above the rest and even went so far as issuing theatre-like programmes for the shows. New front of house staff were employed and dressed in a manner to suit the

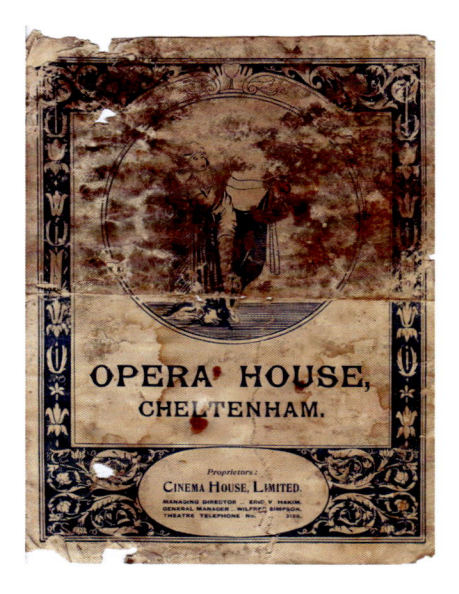

Programme for the film *The Big House* at the Opera House Cinema, 23rd February 1932

A 1930s charabanc outing for members of the Opera House company

pretentions of the smart new establishment. The girl attendants were resplendent in elegant scarlet frocks with blue facings, and the men in uniforms of claret, gold and blue. To add even more class, a page boy was employed as doorman to welcome the patrons to their new and exciting experience. The house lights dimmed and the flickering images were first projected on the 30th September 1929.[5]

The changeover from theatre to cinema at the Opera House was to have far-reaching effects. It had inadvertently created a rather large vacuum in the town for both drama and variety and there were those who were keen to fill it.

In May 1931, Jessie Scrivener, a teacher at the Ladies' College, wrote to the *Echo* suggesting that Cheltenham should follow Bristol's example and establish a repertory company. She suggested that a space in the north wing of the Winter Gardens could easily be converted into a decent theatre.

A couple of months later, in July that year, a meeting was held by the Actors' Church Union at Hatherley Lawn to support the scheme. The local theatre chaplain, the Reverend John Bagshot de la Bere, Vicar of Prestbury, complained light-heartedly that his job had been taken away by the Opera House ceasing to be a theatre. The Mayor, Alderman P. T. Smith spoke of 'a great calamity from the…point of view of trying to attract people to the town'. He said the Council would endorse Miss Scrivener's scheme if the town would support it. He drew attention to a likely candidate to take the job on.[6]

Rex Burchell was an actor-manager of the old-school who had been around a long time. His Warwick Revue had frequently toured to the Far East, often playing the Victoria Theatre in Singapore.[7] In 1930/1 he was in Cheltenham running his *Folly* concert party at the cramped and inadequate Pavilion stage in Montpellier Gardens.[8] In spite of the support of the Mayor, Burchell's application to set up a repertory company in the Winter Gardens was turned down by the Council.

Miss Scrivener's idea was not doomed though. One of her former pupils, Barbara Kent, in partnership with Ernest Cox and his wife Ellen Compton, put in a bid to the Council for the Winter Gardens space. The Council agreed on condition that the new partnership converted the building and paid for lighting, heating and cleaning. Ellen Compton was part of the distinguished theatrical family that included Sir Compton MacKenzie and Fay Compton.[9]

Undeterred, Rex Burchell had found other premises, and in the autumn of 1931 he leased the former cinema in North Street from H. G. Beard, who also owned the Coliseum, and set up the Repertory Theatre.

The building had first opened in 1910 as The Albert Hall which put on various events including plays. It was taken over by the proprietors of the Coliseum, two hundred yards along the road, changing its name in 1911 to the Royal Cinema de Luxe and later to the Theatre of Varieties and Cinema de Luxe. The venture was not without its success and in February 1917 the legendary Dan Leno appeared there in *The Glad Idlers*.

Burchell's Repertory Theatre opened on 23rd November and *The Stage* said, 'The hall is excellently adapted to theatre purposes. The company had a hearty send-off'.[10] A Playgoers' Circle was formed to support the new theatre, but by the following January they were already being asked to dip into their pockets.

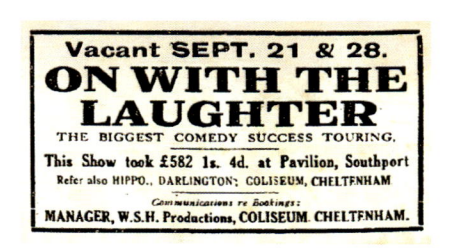

A meeting was called and the Circle was told that the Rep had lost £500 in the first two months and that without support it would be unable to continue. The problem seems to have been caused by the initial outlay in creating the theatre and its small size.[11] Burchell's Repertory Theatre struggled on for another year but was doomed to failure. It was taken over by a couple more companies but it closed for the last time as a theatre in April 1934.[12] The building became a garage and was demolished in 1988.

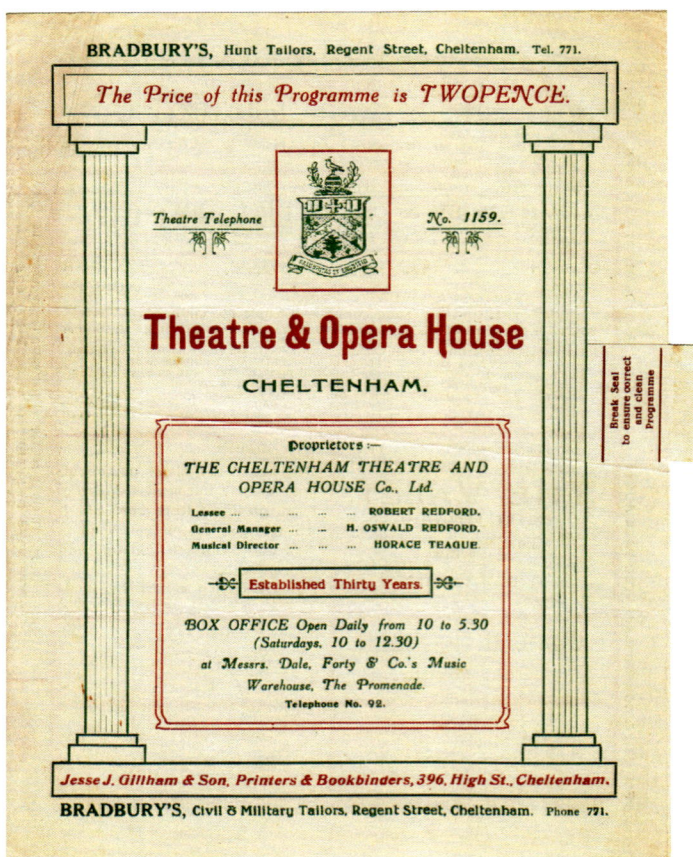

The cinema at the Opera House was, for whatever reason, not a great success; possibly because it tried to present itself as smarter and more exclusive than the other cinemas in town. In 1934, probably taking its cue from the closure in North Street, The Cheltenham Theatre & Opera House Company bought back the Regent Street building and reinstated it as a full-time theatre with Wilfred Simpson as Managing Director.

Immediately after the theatre reverted to its previous owners, another major overhaul was undertaken which lasted five weeks. The first things to go were the twelve cast iron columns that supported the Dress Circle and the boxes. Gilded and painted they were very attractive, unless of course you were sitting behind one of them. The Opera House was re-opened again as a theatre by the Mayor, Cllr. Edward Ward, on Monday 27th August 1934.[13]

After interminable delays, the Winter Garden Theatre finally opened its doors on Monday 9th December 1935 with a production of Norman Ginsbury's *Viceroy Sarah*. The feelings about the improvised theatre were mixed. *The Echo* thought it had 'converted into a very pleasant theatre'.[14] However, the playwright and critic St. John Ervine described it as a 'melancholy hall'.[15] One couldn't help feeling that with such long delays since the scheme was first mooted and the reopening of the Opera House as a theatre the previous year, the Winter Gardens had rather missed the boat.

Another Compton, Jean, was also part of the company along with her husband Arthur Howard. Arthur was the brother of Hollywood star Leslie Howard and father of leading Shakespearian actor Alan Howard.

In January 1935, Wilfred Simpson gave the annual pantomime

luncheon at the Plough Hotel for the directors and company members of the show which had just finished its three week season. *Dick Whittington* had been the eighth Frank Maddox panto to be staged at the Opera House and Simpson proudly told his audience that each of them 'had been more successful than that before it with the result that this season's presentation surpassed all records in the history of the theatre'.[16]

Even though the cinema was becoming more and more popular, there were many for whom a weekly visit to the Opera House was an essential part of life. Graham Teal has fond memories of the theatre from the thirties. 'When I was a child my parents would always take me to the Opera House. They never went to the pictures, only the Opera House. We used to go weekly on a Saturday night, queued up to get into the gods as we called it. We started going in about 1937 I think. I would have been five or six years old. I remember seeing *Twinkle* there, with Clarkson Rose, Hutch and G. H. Elliot who was known as *The Chocolate Coloured Coon*. It was all variety in those days, I don't remember any plays. *Twinkle* use to come for a fortnight and they'd change the show for the second week.'

The Rex Burchell Company 1931

However, Rex Burchell's efforts to create and run a repertory theatre in Cheltenham, along with those of the more successful Winter Gardens company, didn't go unnoticed by the Opera House management. In May 1939 Derek Salberg was invited to bring a rep company to the theatre for a few weeks, opening with *George and Margaret*.

Derek Salberg ran Birmingham's Alexandra Theatre after having taken it over from his father, Leon, the year before. Derek's brother, Reginald, ran the Salisbury rep for many years and along with their other brother, Keith, the Salbergs were stalwarts of regional theatre in England right through until the 1970s.

At the end of Salberg's opening night, the Mayor, Cllr. John Howell, delivered warm words of encouragement and he made a strong appeal to the people of Cheltenham to give the venture the support it deserved.[17]

By the end of Derek Salberg's time in Cheltenham, the Second World War was already underway. Undeterred, the Opera House carried on and, like the Windmill Theatre in London, they never closed. But it was to be twenty years before another sortie into repertory was

KENNETH KENT AS "NAPOLEON"

THE OPERA HOUSE
TELEPHONE 5144 and 5148 (Two Lines)
Managing Director WILFRED SIMPSON

BARRY O'BRIEN and ROY LIMBERT present

FRANCIS L. SULLIVAN as "HERCULE POIROT" in

PERIL AT END HOUSE

By AGATHA CHRISTIE
Adapted by ARNOLD RIDLEY

August 11th
NIGHTLY 7-0
Saturday at 2-30 p.m.

"MURDER WITHOUT CRIME"

EXCITING EVENI...
...ss Agate—Sund...

The Opera House, Cheltenham
TEL. 5144/5

**Dress Circle
Matinee Thursday**
2-15 & 5-0 PM
THURSDAY 4 JAN 1940
4/- including Tax
ROW G SEAT No. 9
To be retained.

THE OPERA HOUSE
TELEPHONE 5144 (Two Lines)
Managing Director WILFRED SIMPSON

PROGRAM...
THE SPECTACULA...

VENUS COMES TO TOWN

ROSEMARY ANDREE

Commencing Monday, March 9th 1942
6-0 — TWICE NIGHTLY — 8-0

THE OPERA HOUSE
TELEPHONE 5144 and 5148 (Two Lines)
Managing Director WILFRED SIMPSON

PROGRAMME

WILFRED SIMPSON presents his
Grand Xmas Pantomime

DICK WHITTINGTON
AND HIS CAT

Commencing Boxing Day, December 26th
for a Short Season
TWICE DAILY — 7-0

Chapter 6

Twinkle and a Naughty Cat
The Opera House at war 1939-1945

In spite of the outbreak of World War Two, it was business as usual in Regent Street. Just a couple of weeks after war was declared in September 1939, Fred Clayton's variety company was in town and top of the bill was a familiar name – Maskelyne.

'Mr. Jasper Maskelyne is the grandson of the original J. N. Maskelyne and in a speech in response to the big reception he and his company received on Monday he mentioned that it was just 100 years ago that his grandfather was born in Cheltenham. The box he had used for the box trick was that with which his grandfather's name was associated and which he had used for the same trick that night.'[1]

At Christmas 1939, Wilfred Simpson produced his first pantomime at the Opera House creating a tradition that would carry on until he retired and sold his shares in the Company in 1955. The following year his second pantomime was *Babes in the Wood*, but the war was already beginning to make things difficult. Cheltenham had already been the victim of a couple of bombings, in November and December, and people now thought twice before venturing out at night. The panto scenery, which was being built in London, was damaged in a raid before it could be delivered and had to be repainted.

And if that wasn't enough, as a result of the air-raids on Cheltenham, the town's Education Committee refused permission for local school children to take part in the pantomime because it would have meant them having to go home during the black-out. Nevertheless, the

Playbill for a *Jane* revue, 1945. These shows, based on the saucy *Daily Mirror* cartoon strip, toured for many years through the 1940s and 50s

show went on and 'in spite of all the difficulties the producer may be congratulated on a very nice piece of work in which local taste has been, as usual, well understood and met'.[2]

Cheltenham's most famous theatrical son was Ralph Richardson. He had been born in Tivoli Road in 1902. He, along with Laurence Olivier and John Gielgud, was the leading actor of his generation. For many years Gielgud ran his own company and in September 1941 came to the Opera House with his production of J. M. Barrie's *Dear Brutus* with a star studded cast that included Roger Livesey, Martita Hunt, Nora Swinburne and Muriel Pavlow.

Super sleuth Hercule Poirot was as popular then as he is now. Agatha Christie's play *Peril at End House* came to Cheltenham in an adaptation written by Arnold Ridley, of *Dad's Army* fame. Later that year a 22-year-old Beryl Reid appeared in the musical *Betty*, a vehicle for Betty Leslie-Smith, which boasted 'gorgeous costumes' and 'beautiful scenery'.

Donald Wolfit, one of the greatest actor-managers of modern times, brought his company to the Opera House in October 1941. He presented *Hamlet, Richard III* and, by special request, *The Merchant of Venice*. The following year he appeared in *David Garrick*, a play about the 18th century actor-manager. In fact, it was Wolfit who was the inspiration for 'Sir' in Ronald Harwood's play *The Dresser* which played the Everyman in 2005 with Nicholas Lyndhurst of *Only Fools and Horses* fame and Julian Glover in the Wolfit part.

During the war it was all about keeping your chin up and, of course, being patriotic. The two were often combined into the dozens of revues that constantly toured the country, picking their way through the blackout, dodging the bombs. In November 1941, Jack Edge presented a new revue entitled *See You in the Shelter*, billed as 'the Funniest and Most Topical and Comedy Revue Touring'. An un-named doctor is quoted as having said 'I could not prescribe a better tonic. I saw the show Monday. It is now Friday and I'm still laughing'.

At the beginning of November, Ernie Lotinga starred in *Sailors Don't Care* 'A Musical Naval Show in Eight Scenes'. Following that, at the beginning of December, Jimmy Mac appeared in 'a new and novel production' at the theatre called *Naughty ! Naughty!* Featuring songs of a patriotic nature including *Raw Recruits, H.M.S. Mighty, On Parade* and *Cockneys on Parade* and stayed on for the pantomime.

The new show, again produced in house by the Opera House manager Wilfred Simpson, was the ever popular *Dick Whittington and his Cat*. Violet Fields starred alongside Jimmy Mac. Mac was a regular visitor to the Opera House and appeared in many pantomimes and revues over the years.

Nancy Shipway-Blackwell has been a regular visitor to the theatre for more than seventy years. She first went as a small child in the late thirties and attended pantomimes throughout the war. She has vivid recollections of the 1941 show and of meeting Dick Whittington's cat. 'We were sitting in the Dress Circle and in the interval they would bring you tea on a tray. The pantomime cat would run around the auditorium and I remember it sitting on the balcony rail pretending to drink our milk. It's funny, because I remember the safety curtain that used to come in during the interval. It had *For Thine Eternal Safety* written on it and they used to have a slide show of adverts for local shops.'

Nancy's uncles, Bill and Ralph Shipway, were dentists with their practice just along the road from the theatre at 16 Regent Street. 'The actors would go there if they needed treatment and I remember the pantomime dame used to say, 'I've got a dreadful tooth-ache, I must go to Shipways'.

OPERA HOUSE
Telephone: 5144-5
Week commencing MONDAY, AUGUST 25th, 1941
6.0 - Twice Nightly - 8.0

ANCASTER THEATRICAL PRODUCTIONS SHOW YOU

SILK STOCKING

SCANDALS OF 1940

THE SHOW FOR MODERN TIMES
Devised and Staged by
Cecil G. Buckingham and Burton Lester
With a Great Cast of 25 Artistes, including

BURTON LESTER
Popular American Entertainer, with his Gang of Comedians

MARK RIVERS | **BILLY BLYTH** | **DANNY KEEN**

GLADYS NEVILLE

THE SIX Princesses of Modern Rhythm
Hiawatha Hotshots

BERTIE STARMER

THE THREE GIRL FRIENDS
KATHLEEN — OLIVE — MAVIS

FORCES TAKE A BOW

BARE BRAND BEAUTIES

The **Cottrillos**
South American Acrobatic Jugglers

THE **Dawn Patrol BALLET**

Perfecta Press, London, S.E.5.

'My father was a farmer at Duntisbourne, near Cirencester and he would come to Cheltenham on Thursday for Market Day. I often went with him and when the market was finished we'd go to the theatre and he'd buy tickets for whatever was on that night. I saw the Crazy Gang and Old Mother Riley and Jimmy Mac who was often in the pantomimes. I still go to the Everyman and I sponsored a seat as part of the fund-raising for the 2011 restoration. The brass plaque says 'Happy Days', which they were.'

Undeterred by the war raging in the skies above England there was a *Grand Pantomime Ball* at the Town Hall on 7th January 1942. Artists from the show performed a cabaret and there was dancing to Billy Gammon and his Band. Billed as *The Night of Nights*, for 4/- (20p) you got all this and a bar and buffet too.

One of the most popular touring shows in England over a period of forty-odd years was Clarkson Rose's *Twinkle*. The show made its debut in 1921 on Ryde Pier. Over the years it made numerous visits to the Opera House right up till the 1960s when it played at the Everyman during the rep's Spring break in May 1962.

While Clarkson Rose was appearing at the Opera House in 1941, he wrote a couple of pieces for *The Stage* which combined praise for Cheltenham and its surroundings along with grumpy old man complaints about everything else. In the first piece headed *PERADVENTURE Being more Leaves from a Pro's Log Book* he wrote:

'Once more back in the beautiful town of Cheltenham, one of the few towns whose character remains unchanged in a world of changing architecture. Whether the City Fathers here have some law about new buildings being made to conform in some way to surrounding architecture, I don't know, but even the mammoth picture houses in certain parts do so. I advise incoming companies to write and fix their accommodation as early as possible, because the digs question is a real problem. Many of the land-ladies who used to let to professionals now turn a deaf ear to them.

'On the Sunday I arrived, I spent hours trying to find accommodation, and in the end had to fall back on a hotel, which, although they had accommodation left, didn't want to take people owing to staff shortage. These are difficult times for everybody, but I do think there are some people in the world who are taking advantage of the fact that there is a war on.

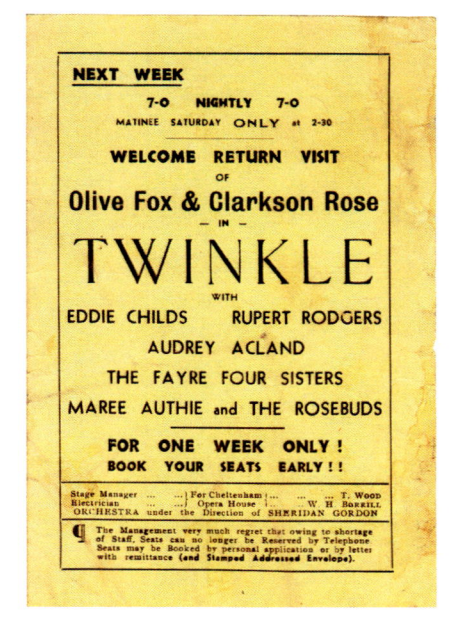

"I blame the theatre managements,' said one well-known artist to me the other day. Well, it's very easy to blame someone, but how can one really blame the theatre managements? They send out lists of apartments, and very often the local stage-manager goes round and does his best. But theatre managements, cannot make landladies answer letters, or even make them give you service if you do find them ready to take you in.

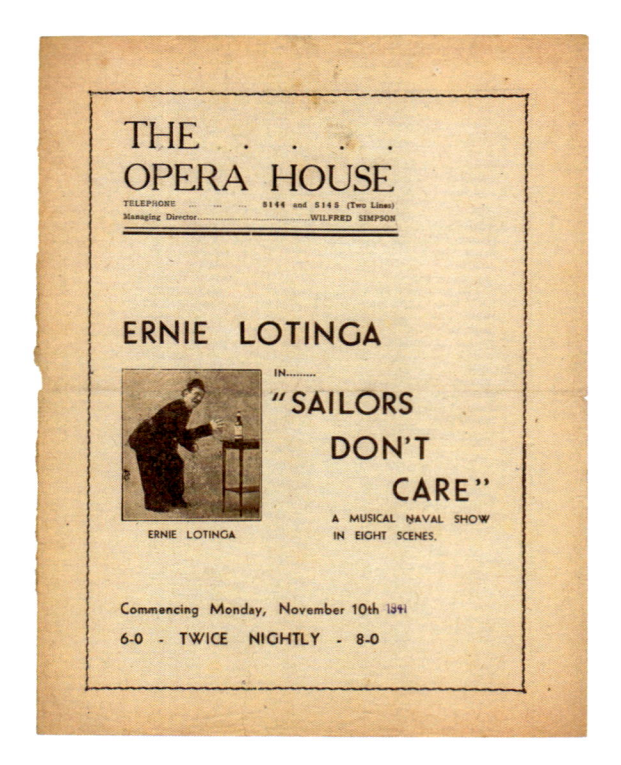

'It is very hard, for people on small salaries to be told, as they often are told today, that the landlady will do them bed and breakfast, and they must get all their other meals out. If meals out can be obtained at prices that are in proportion to the cost and service, it would be a different matter, but they are not'.[3]

A week later, Mr. Rose was again waxing lyrical, but still found lots to complain about. 'These spring days in Cheltenham are very beautiful. How pleasant it is to take a bus from Cheltenham's Promenade to the summit of Cleeve Hill. One can ramble about here for hours and there are glorious views of the surrounding Cotswolds.

'But so much have times changed that when I went for my tea, I found a notice *Residents only served*. This sort of thing is getting pretty frequent and cannot be helped so it is advisable to take refreshment with you on these trips. I tried five places round Cleeve Hill, all of which had their pre-war signs up making us think of crowded gardens, under gaily coloured umbrellas. And another day we go to prettily named Birdlip, which is a beautiful climb the other side of Cheltenham and the woods at the top are well worth a visit. Primroses, polyanthus and wild violets almost made a multi-coloured carpet to walk upon and the chirrups of the birds made you forget the drone of the planes overhead.'

Graham Teal, who visited the Opera House every week night, rain or shine, with his parents, remembers the war. 'We still went there every Saturday right through to the end of the war, it never shut. We were actually in the theatre one of the nights Cheltenham was bombed. The show just carried on as normal and afterwards we just walked home.

'The theatre was always full; it was chock-a-block. I think one of the last shows I saw there at that time was Charlie Chester; he had this tenor called Fred Ferrari. He was a tiny little short man, I couldn't believe it, but when he started singing you could feel the seats vibrating right up in the gallery. He used to be in The Crazy Gang at one time, I believe, but I think *Twinkle* was my favourite show of all of them.'

Monday, March 4th For One Week
Monday to Friday at 7-30 p.m.
Saturday at 5-0 & 8-0 p.m.

...rer Carpenter CHELTENHAM ...OUSE
PHONE—5144

PAUL RAYMOND presents
for and on behalf of FOLIES PARISIENNE LTD.

THE SENSATIONAL FRENCH PLAY

'THE BED'

...itten for English Speaking Audiences by
...AND ED FEILBERT (of America)

...Paris "MOU-MOU" by...

with
PAYNE
...OYLE
...SLER

HOUSE, CHELTENHAM
...LEPHONE 5144
J. W. Simpson
...rector
...istant Manager — Andrew B. Martin

WEEK COMMENCING
MONDAY, DEC. 6th, 1954
6-0 Twice Nightly 8-15

A.D. PRODUCTIONS
presents

HOTTER THAN PARIS

A Heatwave of
...OVELIES and LAUGHS

The Opera House Cheltenham
Tel. 5144
DRESS CIRCLE
First House
6.30 P.M.
SATURDAY...
2/- including Tax
ROW G SEAT No. 6
To be retained

OPERA...
...
Direc...
Assist...

WEEK C...
MONDAY...
6-0   Twice Nig...

BILLIE ROCHE presents

PUT ME AMONG THE GIRLS

The Only
...LL GIRL Revue Touring
with
IRIS

...CHELTENHAM
5144
...ager — Wilfred Simpson
...Andrew B. Martin

COMMENCING
Nov. 23rd - 1953
NIGHTLY 8-15

...and F. J. BUTTERWORTH (Prods.) LTD.
present
The 1953 Coronation Edition of

WINDMILL FOLLIES

SPECTACLE · GLAMOUR · COMEDY
With vocal arrangements by Len Cole and...
Harry Mills. Choreography by...

Lyons
ICE CREAM
KUP
3d

HONKY-TONK

THE BURLESQUE LEG SHOW

Chapter 7

Pantos and Panties
The end of the Opera House 1946-1959

Wilfred Simpson had produced his pantomimes throughout the war without a break. His seventh, the first since the end of hostilities, was *Aladdin*, which *The Stage* described as 'brisk, polished and tastefully dressed. Scott Gordon's and T. E. D. Lewis' humour as Widow Twanky and Wishee-Washee was 'good, quick and rollicking' while Pat Beryl, playing Prince Pekoe, 'had the legs and presence befitting her royal purple'.[1]

The show also demonstrated the importance of specialty acts in pantomime. These 'speshes', as they were known, were what variety acts did at Christmas. They would do a summer season at the end of a pier, months of touring round the halls and finish up in December and January in a nice warm theatre with thousands of excited children. The end of variety also marked the end of pantomime speciality acts, but in 1946, Simpson was still able to find enough acts to punctuate the show; *Aladdin* had Frank Wilson playing the concertina and *Les Cygnes Four* performing their acrobatic act. There was also a ventriloquist and someone playing the banjulele.

By 1947 the theatre was presenting rather more prestigious productions. The Bristol Old Vic company performed *King Lear* starring Kenneth Connor, later to be one of the stalwarts of the *Carry On* films, as the Fool. This was followed by Hatti Jacques and Rupert Davies in the Young Vic production of *The King Stag*. Among the other shows that year were *The Winslow Boy* by Terence Rattigan and a return of John Gielgud's company with his production of Oscar Wilde's *Lady*

Cyril Fletcher was to be a regular visitor to the theatre in Cheltenham, either in revue or, later, as dame in pantomime

Windermere's Fan, but without Gielgud himself. A few months later a revue called *Tuppence Coloured* played Cheltenham starring Joyce Grenfell and Max Adrian.

The following year some fledgling actors were beginning to spread their wings. In May 1948, the theatre presented *Dark Summer*, a long since forgotten play, memorable only for a very early appearance of Richard Burton.

Cyril Fletcher was to become a regular in Cheltenham. One of his first visits was in 1949 in a musical entitled *Magpie Masquerade* which also featured 'the new B.B.C. comedian' Harry Secombe. The perennial Fletcher was to appear in pantomimes at the theatre until the early seventies.

On 27th June 1949 Malcolm Farquhar, who was to become one of the most successful artistic directors of the Everyman rep, played the Opera House in *Twice Upon a Saturday*. A few weeks later a young Roger Moore appeared in R. C. Sherriff's *Miss Mable*, which also starred Arthur Lowe.

However, by September that year there was some indication of the way things were beginning to go. On 12th September a show called *Venus Was a Lady* opened at the Opera House featuring Rosemary (Venus) Andree billed as 'the Most Glamorous Nude'. This show was to mark the start of a trend in touring girlie shows that was to last right through the 1950s and reduce many once respectable venues to little more than seedy flea pits. But it was, ironically, that decline that often led to the renaissance of the British theatre and the growth and importance of the repertory system that was to dominate the provincial theatre for over two decades. In fact it was to inspire John Osborne to write one of his best plays, *The Entertainer*.

On 12th March 1950, Rosemary Andree brought her show, *French Follies,* to the Opera House and by 1951 the trend for saucy, burlesque type shows was well established. *Mesdemiselles* [sic] *from Armentiers… Parlez Vous?* which opened on 6th August was billed as 'a real French Revue' and featured comedian Bernie Winters who, with his brother Mike, would become an enormous television star a decade later.

The stream of tawdry revues was now becoming a torrent. The very next show after *Mesdemiselles* was *Bon Soir Mesdames* described as 'a real French Frolic'. Straight drama was now becoming rare but in May and June 1952 there was a string of decent plays including *Ring Around the Moon* by Jean Anouilh.

It was in the early fifties that actor Stephen Boswell made his first visit to the theatre. 'It must have been Christmas 1951 when the acting bug bit me. I was four and taken to the pantomime at the Opera House by my nanny. Afterwards we went backstage to have tea with Sylvia Addison, the principal dancer. My mother, Margaret Davies, ran the Ellenborough Hotel in Oriel Road where a lot of the actors from the theatre stayed and where I had made friends with Sylvia. After the matinee of *Little Red Riding-Hood*, we walked across the stage where stage-hands were repairing a large bed. When I asked what they were doing, one of them informed me that they were mending the sheets because the Wolf had ripped them with his claws. I squeezed my nanny's hand tighter and hoped that the Wolf was locked up and far away'.

Brian Ward worked in the old Opera House back in 1952. 'As a lad I never went to the theatre but I used to collect autographs and I'd to hang around the stage door. I got to know Jeff Jones who was the stage-manager in those days; he was a really nice man'. Jeff Jones was married to Valantyne Napier, *The Human Spider* who appeared in several pantomimes at the Opera House, most notably as the Spider in *Little Miss Muffet*.

Brian Ward continued, 'Jeff suggested I worked there backstage when I left school and so, when I left All Saints School at 15, that's where I went. My first day at work was the first time I had ever stepped into a theatre. It was a totally different world, it was dreamland. Working there took up nearly all my time. I had virtually no life outside of the Opera House'.

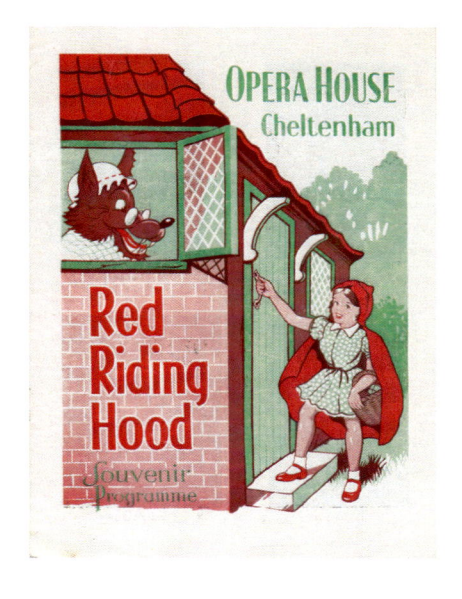

Chapter 7 Pantos and Panties

The theatre in November 1959 presenting *Call Me Madam* by the CODS – the very last show before the Opera House closed

Obviously, as the most junior member of staff, life in the theatre for Brian was not always glamorous. 'As day boy I was the lowest of the low. My duties included turning off the old gas lighting and sweeping the stage; all the menial jobs, but I loved it. I used to get sent up to Doris's café in Pittville Street to collect two great big jugs of tea and some dripping cakes for all the stage-hands.'

But working backstage during the girlie shows was not without its benefits, as Brian remembers. 'The show based on *Jane* from the *Daily Mirror* cartoon strip was very popular. Very tame by today's standards but for a lad of fifteen in the 1950s it was quite an eye opener. One of my jobs was to 'walk' the tabs across to make sure they closed properly and grab the other one because if they bounced open you could see the semi-naked girls moving around behind and that wasn't allowed. But it didn't stop me seeing them. But the shows were quite respectable; they weren't what you'd call seedy. I got the impression it was just normal audiences, not men in dirty macs.'

Another young lad who got a job backstage was 16-year-old Dennis Herbert who went to work at the theatre in 1954. 'My job was to help with the stage lighting even though I had no experience at all. My boss's name, the electrician, was Mr. Rayburn. Another of my jobs was to help put up the scenery on a Sunday afternoon. The old horse and cart would have brought it down from the station and we had to put it up with all the lights and stuff.'

One of Dennis' main jobs was one of the most unpleasant in the theatre. "On the limes' meant being perched high in the gods, operating the spotlights that followed the actors on the stage far below. Lime lights were in fact gas lights and had first been used in Covent Garden in 1837. The lamps were now electric of course and more correctly called arc lights but the old name persisted and gave rise to the expression 'being in the limelight'. 'These lamps used to get really hot and dirty and you had to change the gels, the coloured filters, all the time and every ten minutes you had to adjust the carbon which gave off the light. All this while handling this near red hot lamp with just a little wooded handle.

'The actors would often ask me to run over to the old Plough Hotel to get them drinks for the interval. I also remember lots of nice girls in the chorus of the pantomime. We used to get free cinema passes so we'd take the girls to the pictures in the afternoon, before the show.'

Lew and Leslie Grade were also producing touring variety shows at the time and on 10th August 1953 presented 'The Dynamic Singing Personality of Radio and Television' Betty Driver, later to become a star of *Coronation Street*, plus full variety company at the Opera House.

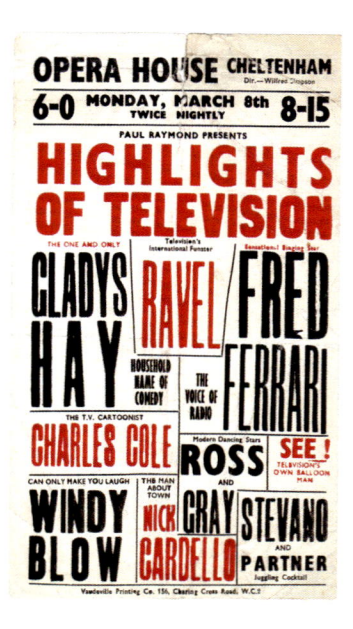

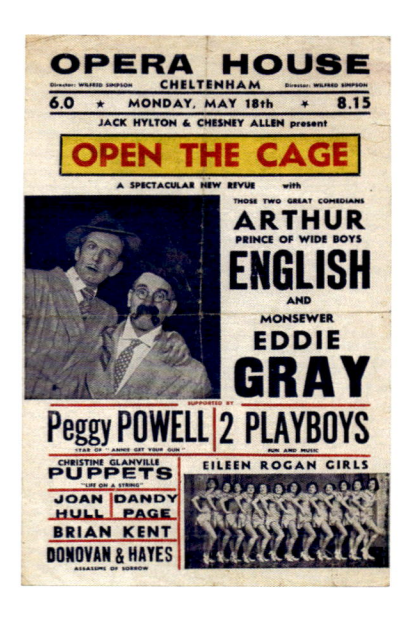

1953 was of course the year of the Coronation and lots of shows were keen to jump on the royal bandwagon. Cyril Fletcher returned in September with his *Coronation Masquerade* which was followed in November by *The Coronation Edition of Windmill Follies*. In fact, one of Brian Ward's duties was as Cyril Fletcher's dresser. 'He used to send me across the road to the old Star for his double gin and tonic every night.'

By 1954, television was beginning to influence what was on at the theatre. In fact, there were those in the profession who firmly believed that the Coronation marked the start of theatre's decline. Hundreds of thousands, if not millions, of people bought their first television set in order to watch the event. Once it was installed in pride of place in their living room, they were reluctant to switch it off.

There has been a tendency in recent years for shows to feature soap-stars or to be based on television shows but, like most things, that's nothing new. In May 1954, a stage version of *The Archers* was presented at the Opera House, but it was a return to the status quo when a week later *Honky-Tonk, The Burlesque Leg Show* enthralled audiences with turns by The Britvic Lovelies and 'ace showman' Bob Grey.

It's difficult to imagine what still, staid, old Cheltenham made of these shows. There were clearly enough retired colonels around who were interested in 'art' to buy some tickets, but it was hardly family entertainment.

John Parsons was 17 when he was taken on at the Opera House in 1955. 'I did all sorts of jobs. Sometimes I was up on the limes, other times I was up in the flies and sometimes scene shifting on stage.

'I worked on one of the *Jane* shows. There were about fifteen scenes in the show, or tableaux as they used to call them. Of course in those days the girls weren't allowed to move and in one scene the girl playing Jane had to be chained to a wooden cross, don't ask me why. Anyway, I had to dash on stage between scenes and arrange these chains over her scantily clad body while she lay on this cross. Well, I must have done it too quickly because just as the curtains opened she toppled over on to the floor. I'll always remember that, absolutely fantastic. And, of course, we got fifteen shillings for the Saturday night get out. They were great times, great times.'

But even the straight plays were often forced to present themselves as something exciting or risqué. In August 1955, even the Jean Cocteau play *Bacchus* was translated as *Intimate Relations* and billed as a 'Sensational Story of Life in Paris.'

There was no getting away from it. This was the time of Brigitte Bardot and Jeanne Moreau when anything French was considered to

BOROUGH OF CHELTENHAM

THE WORSHIPFUL THE MAYOR
(ALDERMAN LT.-COL. C. W. BIGGS, O.B.E.)
requests the pleasure of the company of

P. Carpenter Esq

at a
LUNCHEON
to be held at
THE TOWN HALL, on MONDAY, 31st OCTOBER, 1955,
being the first day on which the
CHELTENHAM THEATRE AND OPERA HOUSE
will open under the management and ownership of the Borough Council.

R.S.V.P.: The Mayor's Secretary,
Municipal Offices,
Cheltenham.

12.30 for 1.0 p.m.

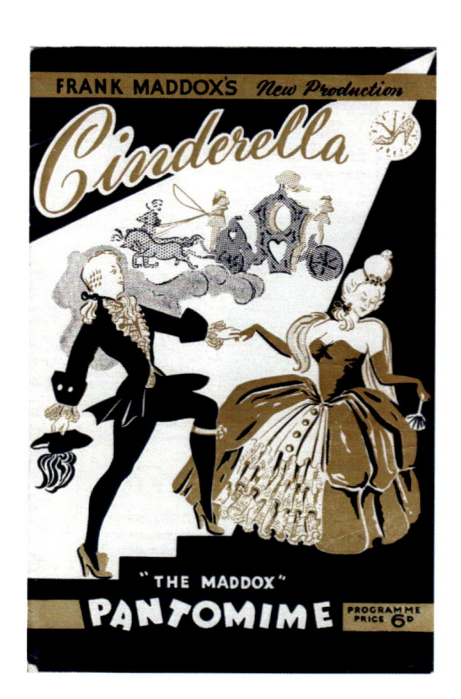

be sexy and stylish. As well as the theatre, virtually every film made in England during this period had to feature a minor French actress to attract the crowds. In fact, if Jean Cocteau and Jean Anouilh hadn't been French, they probably wouldn't have got their plays put on in England at all.

Despite all the tits, bums and saucy French revues, the old theatre management called it a day in 1955; a situation which was almost certainly pre-empted by the long running illness of managing director Wilfred Simpson who had run the Opera House for nearly 30 years.

The Theatre was temporarily reprieved when it was bought in October 1955 by the Cheltenham Corporation for £23,661. To mark the acquisition, a grand lunch was given at the Town Hall at the beginning of November by the Mayor, Lt. Colonel C. W. Biggs, OBE.

Opera House board member J. P. Holborow, while welcoming the council's action, was defensive, claiming, 'We never had a losing year' to people who had insinuated that the Corporation had purchased 'a dead horse'. He revealed that in the previous 21 years, the yearly average profit was £4,990, and the profit in the last year to March 1955, was £4,100. He also claimed that his company could have got a higher price for the building from another source but without the certainty of it continuing as a theatre.[2]

The 1950s was an era when Cheltenham was still thought of as an old folk's home for retired colonels, a situation Colonel Biggs was happy to acknowledge. In his speech at the luncheon he said, 'You may think me old fashioned, but I am all for retired colonels. They are surely all men of tried experience.'[3] He went on, 'There are ill informed people who have sneered at the Council for buying what they considered to be a white elephant. I want to contradict them and to say that the Council have bought an undertaking which, under the management of the directors and the leadership of Mr. Simpson, has shown a material profit'.[4]

The guest of honour was Peter Ustinov who, referring to himself as a 'retired private', said that it was a 'frightfully important occasion, not only for Cheltenham but for the whole of Great Britain'.

On the following Monday 7th November, seventy members of the Cheltenham Borough Council attended a performance in their newly acquired theatre of *Dear Charles* by Alan Melville. The show was produced by Derek Salberg and starred one of the country's most popular entertainers, Jessie Matthews.[5]

Wilfred Simpson's last act as manager of the Opera House had been to negotiate its sale to the council. Not only was he negotiating away his working life but his home at number 10 Regent Street as well. But his main concern was to save the building as a working theatre. In this, as with his many years running the Opera House, he was successful. He died after a long illness on 12th June 1956.

Peter Carpenter was appointed General Manager of the new venture, but during the eighteen months he and the Council ran it, the theatre continued to lose money, maybe because no attempt was made to change the losing formula.

In fact, Alderman H. T. Bush had indicated that things were probably not going to get much better when, at the Town Hall luncheon, he informed everyone that the Council were not acquiring the theatre through any policy of uplift or giving the public what they *ought* to want. They were going, he hoped, to cater for all tastes. 'I am an unreformed lowbrow', he proudly boasted, 'and I shall ensure that I am catered for.'[6]

But not everyone was aware of the problems and many people just enjoyed being there. Iris Bailey worked at the Opera House as an usherette in 1956. 'I was still at school and it was our way of making some pocket money while we studied for our O-Levels. My friend Charlotte Jones and I used to take our school work and once the show had started we'd to go into the ladies toilet in the Dress Circle and do our revision. It was quite nice in those days with a velvet chair and nice carpet and we used to lie on the floor with all our books spread out.

'Usheretting was different in those days. We didn't just used to stand at the door, we took everybody to their seat. You can imagine it was quite slow, but there were quite a few of us working there, including my mother.'

But for Charlotte, working at the Opera House was to have life-changing significance. 'One evening that I still vividly remember, was in November 1956. Next to the last plush red seat in the back row of the Dress Circle was a wooden fold-down seat for the usherette to sit on. One evening a gentleman on the end seat had spread his coat and scarf across it. He quickly realised why I was standing there and apologised profusely, hastily removing his coat and scarf, and I sat down. I recognised him as someone who regularly bought chocolate ice-creams from me in the intervals.

'After the show he was waiting outside and asked me if he could escort me home. He accompanied me to the bus stop. Little did this schoolgirl realise that this lovely man, John, was going to be my future husband and life long soul mate. After I lost my beloved husband in April 2010, I found the original ticket that I had torn in half for him

Frank Maddox

Malcolm Farquhar in 1949

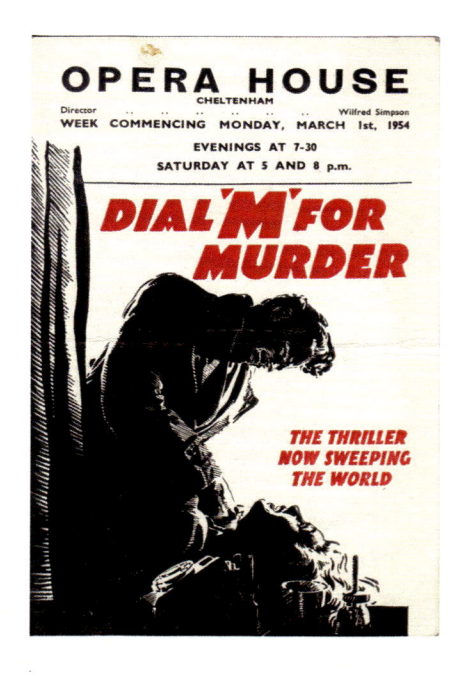

on that very night, November 17th 1956. He had carefully kept it in a metal tin in his drawer, together with a photo of me. The last show that we ever went to together was an opera at the Everyman Theatre on Thursday April 8th 2010, three days before he died.

'Coincidentally, our eldest daughter, Rachel Jones, was communications and marketing manager of the Everyman between 1997 and 2000. It seems a strange and happy coincidence and builds a kind of affinity with this theatre.'

The Council finally gave up and managed to off-load the theatre by leasing it to a new company headed by Frank G. Maddox. The new Cheltenham Theatre and Opera House Co. Ltd. took over in July 1957 with Maddox as Managing Director. After a two week closure, during which time Maddox put in place his new administration, the Opera House re-opened with a production of *The Reluctant Debutante* by William Douglas Home.

The new regime was an immediate success. A piece in *The Stage* said there were queues at the box office all week and quoted Maddox as claiming that sales were 'far in excess of anything the Opera House has done for many years'.[7]

Maddox was certainly trying to restore a little respectability to the Opera House and he soon invited the Midland Theatre Company to present a short season of plays which included *Separate Tables*, *The Teahouse of the August Moon* and *Random Harvest*.

But the underlying problems refused to go away. On 27th April 1959, in another last ditch attempt to save the theatre, John Gordon Ash was re-engaged as Director of Productions. His brief was to create a new season of plays, a season which represented a completely new policy and direction for the beleaguered theatre. Ash's stated aims were, 'To bring back to the Opera House all those who have hitherto found the programmes too routine and un-enterprising, especially the younger generation without whose support the theatre cannot survive much longer'.

He also stated his intention of presenting a more varied programme of plays 'to include the work of world famous dramatists, thus giving Cheltenham an opportunity to see the sort of professional drama normally associated with London, Birmingham, Oxford, Stratford, Liverpool, Glasgow, Edinburgh and Manchester'.

So now, for the first time in its history, the Opera House was controlling its own professional company and Ash proudly outlined his new, progressive season. It was to include Arthur Miller's *All My Sons*, *Flowering Cherry* by Robert Bolt, John Osborne's *The Entertainer* (a play about an ageing comedian working in seedy provincial girlie shows) and *Tea and Sympathy* by Robert Anderson.

The Stage was impressed. 'John Gordon Ash's company at Cheltenham have settled down during their first month to a steady and artistically encouraging season.' They also liked his choice of plays. 'Frank Shelley joined the company last week to play Archie Rice in *The Entertainer*. This was a fine performance, brash, vital, buoyant, full of subtly observed touches …The play, as a whole was presented racily and with verve.'[8]

This was indeed audacious programming but it was far too ambitious and sophisticated for a conservative, provincial town like Cheltenham, whose theatrical diet for the past decade had been based on easily digestible variety shows and skimpily clad ladies. Despite their best efforts the rot was already too well established and the Opera House was in terminal decline. During its last eight weeks the theatre played to an average of only 20% capacity, attendances in one week being as low as 9% – a mere 527 people.[9]

Derek Malcolm, the former theatre critic of *The Gloucestershire Echo* and film critic of *The Guardian,* felt that, paradoxically, Ash made a big contribution to the theatre's survival. 'It was his season of plays, which ironically closed the old theatre, that psychologically opened the new one. They didn't make money but they created that even more valuable commodity – enthusiasm. It was, in retrospect, a ludicrously ambitious list … but it worked wonders on the mind and taught us why we wanted a new and better theatre in place of the old.'[10]

But the Opera House had finally run out of steam. Frank Maddox invoked his get-out clause and threw in the towel. When the curtain came down on the last performance of Miller's *A View from the Bridge* on 13th June 1959, it was the end of the road that could be seen. The theatre closed a week later with little prospect of ever re-opening. There was talk of it being sold to Cavendish House, Cheltenham's largest and smartest department store, to be used as a furniture warehouse or, even more ignominiously, being turned into a newfangled supermarket.

There was a short and temporary reprieve in November that year when the Cheltenham Operatic and Dramatic Society staged Irving Berlin's *Call Me Madam*.

Surprisingly, a public that had not shown any great interest nor demonstrated any willingness to support the Opera House in its hour of need did not want to see it disappear for ever. Such was the public outcry that only nine short months later the theatre would be reborn under a new name, The Everyman.

THE EVERYMAN THEATRE

APRIL 13
ANNE KENNEDY
ESMOND KNIGHT
A PIECE
OF SILVER

Chapter 8

Everyman for himself
A new era in Regent Street 1959-1961

The public outcry that followed the theatre's closure resulted in the creation of a new public body, The Cheltenham Theatre Association. Its founders were David Phillips, who worked in the Russian department at GCHQ and Margaret Davies who ran the Ellenborough Hotel in Oriel Road.

Derek Malcolm remembered it well. 'One of those fired into action by that extraordinary final season at the Opera House was Margaret Davies. What we would have done without her in those early days I, for one, shall never know. She lobbied and lobbied and lobbied. No one who could be useful escaped her attentions. No one who was useful failed to receive her hospitality. I don't know what patrons of the Ellenborough thought of us as we scurried hither and thither, plotting interminably.'

Mrs. Davies' son, Stephen Boswell, was a 14-year-old Cheltenham College schoolboy at the time but was aware of what was happening. 'My mother was instrumental in saving Matcham's beautiful theatre from becoming a warehouse for Cavendish House. She called a meeting with David Phillips, Derek Malcolm and Phil Jones from the *Gloucestershire Echo* plus John Gordon Ash, the Opera House's last artistic director'.

CHELTENHAM THEATRE ASSOCIATION

URGENT – WANTED £3,000 AT ONCE

TO RE-OPEN
CHELTENHAM OPERA HOUSE
Our only Professional Theatre

£3,000 MUST BE RAISED THIS MONTH

We are HALF-WAY there. Please help us finish the job by taking or sending donations to: Mrs. E. M. Davies, Hon. Sec., Ellenborough Hotel, Oriel Road (just beyond Town Hall) Cheltenham

A. E. Errington, Printer, Cheltenham

On 18th June 1959 a deputation consisting of Phillips and Mrs. Davies, though led by a former chairman of the Chamber of Commerce, Mr. W. Talvan Rees, presented itself to the Mayor and representatives of the Council. Mrs. Davies told *The Echo* after the meeting, 'Our plans are of necessity only in a formative stage at the moment, but we feel that in the future we may need all the help we can get and would like to be in the position to contact everyone who is in a position to help us. Our object is to do everything in our power to keep Cheltenham's professional theatre alive and to ensure a progressive and forward looking policy in the future should the Opera House's closure be only temporary'.[1]

In August the Association called a public meeting to rally support for the campaign. In spite of a newspaper strike, which made publicising the event difficult, 500 people turned up at the Shaftesbury Hall to hear what the campaigners had to say. At the end of the meeting they voted unanimously that the Corporation should be made an offer and that an appeal to raise an initial £3000 should be launched. Half of that was raised within days, although David Phillips warned of complacency as he believed the Council would make its final decision on 21st September.

Unfortunately, not all members of the Council were sympathetic. At the Council meeting on 8th September, the deputy Mayor, Charles Irving, was criticised for saying that events had shown that the public did not want a theatre that they would have to subsidise. He was sternly condemned by Alderman D. L. Lipson for making remarks which he described as 'detrimental to the efforts of the Cheltenham Theatre Association'.

Irving, who was later to become Mayor of Cheltenham and its Member of Parliament said afterwards, 'Personally I feel, and I think a good many members feel, that whilst one must applaud the work that the Theatre Association has been trying to do in encouraging the public in preserving the theatre, I still feel it will have to take further measures if the Council is to consider an offer and it will have to take a much more realistic attitude about running this as a theatre.

'We have our Civic Theatre [The Playhouse] which is an expense to the local authority – but it is very well run and a worthy institution. But I cannot agree in my own mind that it would be right and proper for the Council to say that they will subsidise The Opera House in order to keep it open for a small section of the public who wish to use it. If there was a public demand, why is it shutting? Why is it in the financial position it is in today? It is in that position simply because the people in Cheltenham have not supported it. They can see top shows and artists on television and at larger theatres in nearby districts, of top-class quality.'

A second public meeting was held at St. Mary's Hall on 28th October 1959 to introduce the new board of directors and to announce that they aimed to re-open the theatre the following Easter. The meeting was addressed by Cyril Wood O.B.E,[2] the Association's new General Administrator who told the audience, 'Forget everything you have heard or think about the Opera House. This is something completely new to Cheltenham'.

Margaret Davies

The Association, spearheaded by the joint efforts of David Phillips and Margaret Davies, secured financial backing from the Arts Council and negotiated with Cheltenham Corporation to re-open the theatre. The Council eventually granted the Association a three years lease at £1,000 per year commencing on 1st December 1959. Cyril Wood said, 'It required an act of faith on their part no less than ours to grant us a three year lease when they might have yielded to more tempting commercial offers'.[3]

At this point it was clear that the original estimate of £3,000 was

The Big Classical at Cheltenham College

not enough and it was now thought that £5,000 was the minimum amount needed for the theatre to re-open at Easter 1960, and that a further £10,000 would be needed in the first year for running costs. At the time of the October public meeting the Association had already been given £1,467, promised a further £1,255 and had guarantees for over £1,000.[4]

On 6th December 1959 the theatre re-opened its doors, for the very last time as The Opera House for a gala fund raising performance entitled *Meet Your Friends*.

Among the performers was Julian Slade, whose family home was in nearby Painswick. He had strong links with the Old Vic in Bristol, which had premiered his musical *Salad Days* which opened in 1954 and played 2,282 performances in the West End grossing over £700,000. Slade was committed to the survival of the theatre and in order to avoid its immediate demise in 1959, had put on a show in September that year at the Big Classical Theatre at the Cheltenham College which raised £150 for the appeal.

The back of the theatre seen from the Plough Hotel. The car park and hotel is now the site of the Regent Arcade.

Funding also came from a prestigious, international source. It was in this period that the theatre's youth and educational programmes began, when in 1959 the Gulbenkian Foundation gave £2,000 to convert facilities for the fledgling Young Everyman Group.

A young local architect, Derek Whitestone, was called in to modernise the façade and front of house facilities and the auditorium was also refurbished. However not every detail was thought through and some important details were left to others.

David Palmer had been coming to the theatre since 1939 when his mother regularly brought him to see the shows on a Saturday night, perched high in the gods. In 1960 he was working for the sign-writers, Priestley Studios, in Gloucester and remembers how that company was largely responsible for the appearance of the new theatre.

'When they were trying to raise money to get the Everyman open, lots of local businesses offered their support. My boss, John Priestley, lived in Cheltenham and offered to put up the new canopy for them. He said he wanted me to put up a sign to go on the front of the canopy. I chose a type face called *Playbill* which, as the name suggests, was a sort of classic type for posters and the like. So, I drew up and cut these letters out in Perspex and stuck them up on the bright yellow canopy. Anyway, that's how it came about. There was no designer or anything; we more or less made it up ourselves. And that typeface and the yellow were used on everything for years afterwards'.

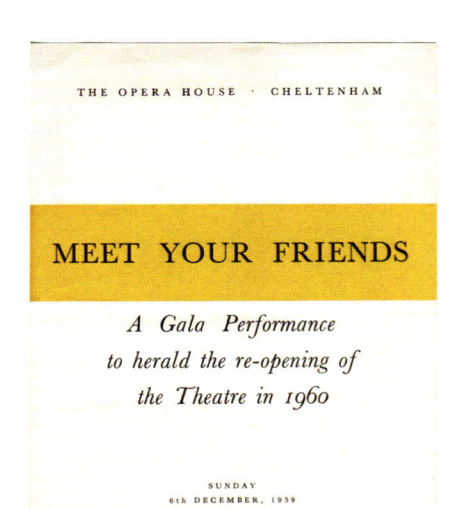

To even the casual passer-by these changes would have been very obvious as they necessitated, for the first time, completely changing the building's façade to accommodate 'modern' features. This involved a lot of straight lines, plate glass and garish colours. The front of house was also substantially revamped, again aiming at a trendy, contemporary look.

It is understandable that the new management wanted to shake off the old Victorian image of the Opera House and, of course, they wanted to be modern. The problem with 'modern' is that it sooner or later becomes old-fashioned. The style of the Everyman's sixties façade owed a great deal to the modernism of the fifties and consequently, by the mid-seventies, was already showing its provenance.

The transformation was achieved at remarkable speed and now The Everyman Theatre Company, with its new policy of fortnightly repertory, was ready for business. The first season at the newly named theatre opened 2nd May 1960 with a production of N. C. Hunter's *A Piece of Silver*. The programme for that production contained the following explanation for the change to the theatre's name:

'… A new name seemed essential. The old name 'Opera House' was misleading as an indication of what could be expected inside; it also conjured up the spirit of the late nineteenth century when the theatre was built. The theatre of today must look forward, not back. It must reflect the spirit of today, and today is the age of everyman – so, there was the new name – The Everyman.'

Cheltenham was not alone in choosing that name for its cultural heart. The Everyman Theatre in Hampstead opened in 1920 with high socialist ideals and later became one of the first alternative, independent cinemas in London. Liverpool picked the same name in 1964 for its new, progressive theatre company based in Hope Street and the Everyman amateur dramatic society in Cardiff dates back to the 1940s.

There was a buzz to the word around that time; it captured the *zeitgeist*. It implied equality and egalitarianism which is just what the angry, socialist young men of kitchen-sink drama were promoting. Modern theatre in Britain had become decidedly and proudly left wing.

However, in Cheltenham the Everyman was just a name. There were no political ideals, no lofty ambitions, just a desire to keep a working theatre in the town. The plays it was to present were typical of most reps at the time, still owing more to Noël Coward than Leon Trotsky. Nevertheless, it was live theatre and it was a respectable theatre that no longer needed to rely on tits and bums or the word 'French' to entice audiences through its doors.

The Times, writing about the new company, said, 'The management has set itself an ambitious programme. A scheme for interchange of plays is being arranged with the Belgrade Theatre, Coventry, the Arts Theatre, Cambridge and the Oxford Playhouse and it is hoped eventually to bring other theatres into the circuit'.

Local businessman Noel Newman became the first Chairman of the Board of Directors of the Everyman as well as being Chairman of the Association. Newman had his finger in many local pies and was also President of the Literary Festival Society. Nicola Bennett described him as a most pleasant man and ideal chairman who had the gift of getting things done with the gentlest of urging.[5] Over the years the Everyman was to become a regular venue for Literature Festival events.

For the first year or so the theatre operated its own rep company under the artistic directorship of Peter Powell alongside exchange productions. The first of these visiting companies was from Coventry who presented Oliver Goldsmith's *She Stoops to Conquer,* directed by Clifford Williams, on 23rd May 1960.

In spite of their common aim, the two theatres could not be more different; Cheltenham, a fine old Matcham Victorian building steeped in history, and The Belgrade, in its time, one of the most modern and progressive theatres in Britain. What they shared was that they had both risen from the ashes – literally in the case of the Belgrade which had been built in 1958 to replace the Coventry theatre that was destroyed in the blitz.

Tudor Williams, who would go on to have a lifelong relationship with the Everyman, had also just got a new job. 'I came to Cheltenham in March 1960 to work for the old Black & White coach company. I could hardly believe my luck when I read in the *Gloucestershire Echo* that the new Everyman Theatre was opening in May'.

Jim Lightstone worked in the new Everyman's first rep company. 'I'd just finished my National Service and got a job at the theatre as assistant carpenter. My boss was the stage carpenter, Sam Wakefield. I worked there full time building the scenery. I would sometimes work on a show up in the flies and I usually worked on Saturday nights

The Ellenborough Hotel in Oriel Road

doing the strike and the get out – taking down the old set. I liked that because you'd get cash in hand on top of your normal wages'.

Despite its shaky foundations, the theatre's policy was nothing if not adventurous. In its first six months it staged no less than six world premieres plus the first provincial presentation of Harold Pinter's *The Birthday Party,* which starred Pinter himself, appearing under his stage name of David Baron, alongside Patrick Magee.

Julian Slade, with his writing partner Dorothy Reynolds and her husband Angus MacKay, became important figures in the early rep days in Cheltenham. The Slade/Reynolds 1954 musical *Salad Days* held the record for the longest running West End musical until it was overtaken by Lionel Bart's *Oliver* eleven years later. *Wildest Dreams* was written especially for the Everyman and premiered at the end of October 1960. It was full of 'in' jokes and local references. Cheltenham was 'Nelderham' and Cheltenham's surrounding hills, Cleeve and Leckhampton, became 'Clumpington Hill'.

Stephen Boswell recalls, 'My mum was Mrs. Birdview – 'a lady well known for her cultural activities'. Mrs. Birdview's niece, Carol, was named after my sister Caroline. Angus MacKay was the local composer and 'Stephen Bent' was named after me.' Dorothy and Julian stayed at the Ellenborough while writing the musical. 'In Mrs. Birdview's drawing-room artistic people meet' was the Garden Room where mum had her parties for the Everyman companies.' The show starred Dorothy Reynolds herself, her husband Angus MacKay, Denis Quilley and a young Edward Hardwicke.

Josephine Tewson, who joined the rep in 1961, remembers Margaret Davies and the Ellenborough well. 'We had lots of hospitality at the Ellenborough Hotel. Margaret was very, very generous to us all. She used to phone up and say, 'I've got all these sandwiches left over, come round after the show and eat them up.' Looking back at it, that was nonsense. She'd had the kitchen make up all this food for us specially. We'd all go round and there were all these enormous silver trays piled high with sandwiches and things. We used to all go there quite often, it was very handy for the theatre. And there was also a piano which Lionel Thomson used to play.'

In spite of his lofty aspirations, Peter Powell's time as Artistic

Left: Roland Curram and Andrew Ray in *A Chance in the Daylight*, May 1960

Right: Steven Berkoff in the late 1960s
Photo: Michael Hasted

Dorothy Reynolds and Ralph Nossek in
Not in the Book, 1960
photo: Gerald Pates, Gloucester

Director was not considered a success and he left in February 1961. Nevertheless, David Phillips had some kind words to say about him. 'Mr. Powell resigned because he considered that by then he would have finished the job he had originally set himself, that of getting the theatre on its feet. Mr. Powell wanted to make way for a younger man and to concentrate on writing.'[6] Powell was replaced in March 1961 by 34-year-old David Giles.

One of his first plays at the Everyman was Thornton Wilder's *The Matchmaker* featuring a young Steven Berkoff. It also featured one of the company's ASMs at the time, Windsor Davies, who went on to achieve fame starring in the BBC comedy series *It Ain't Half Hot Mum* between 1974 and 1981.

Berkoff was to appear in several more plays over the next few months including *A Question of Fact* and the Everyman's first birthday production, in May 1961 *Thieves' Carnival*.

Steven Berkoff has very fond memories of his time in Cheltenham. 'I spent four months at the Everyman in the summer of 1961 and performed in some wonderful plays. I remember I played Oberon in the *Midsummer Nights Dream* and I was in *The Matchmaker* and *The Aspern Papers* by Michael Redgrave.

'It was a memorable time for me and very enjoyable. I met some very interesting people.' But he couldn't remember where he lived. 'I wish I could remember where my digs were but they were just round the corner from the theatre and had lovely big, sun-filled rooms. They were wonderful times.'

No matter how nice the digs, it was sometimes nice to get home for a break. So, after the show, one Saturday night, Berkoff set off. 'I remember trying to hitchhike back to London one weekend and people just weren't stopping. I ended up walking all the way to Oxford.'

However, and very disappointingly, the first eleven months of the new Everyman had not been an outstanding success; certainly not financially. On 7th April 1961, Noel P. Newman, chairman of the Board and President of the ETA was obliged to go, cap in hand, to Association members only eighteen months after the original appeal, to again save the theatre from closure. His letter was nothing if not forthright. If it was designed to shock members out of their complacency, it certainly did the trick. It got straight to the point declaring, 'When the move was afoot to re-open the old Opera House many local residents asked themselves whether the people of Cheltenham wanted a theatre and, in the light of actual experience since The Everyman was launched, I ask myself this same question with a deeper and growing concern.

'I realise that my colleagues and I, in the course of operating the theatre, have made errors and misjudgements, either from inexperience or a lack of appreciation of the position. I am, however, convinced that since we appointed David Giles as our Director of Productions we have been offering really first-class theatre in all its aspects. David is a man of boundless enthusiasm and he is backed by an equally energetic and keen Company.'

His summing up was short and didn't pull its punches. 'This is your (and my) last chance to keep The Everyman Theatre in being and I do urge you, not only to come regularly to the theatre yourself, but to persuade your friends and acquaintances that the theatre is really worth visiting and supporting.'

In spite of the positive and encouraging words from Noel Newman, David Giles' days were numbered. His time in charge was to prove even shorter than Peter Powell's, his style and choice of plays being considered a little too high-brow, a proposition confirmed by poor attendances. His reign was to last only three months and he left Cheltenham in May 1961. Nevertheless, in 1970 at the time of Everyman's tenth anniversary he said, 'Whatever I do now or wherever I go, there'll always be a part of me left in the Everyman'.

The financial crisis continued. During the summer of 1961 the theatre owed over £14,000 and, had it not been for the understanding and good will of the creditors, the theatre would not have reopened at all.

After Giles' departure, the theatre was closed for a few months, ostensibly for the 'usual summer recess' but in fact because a huge debt had built up as well as a pile of unpaid bills. In August 1961 all the creditors met to discuss the matter and, as a result, established a moratorium.

The moratorium ran for a year at a time and every August there was a meeting of creditors to vote on whether the theatre could carry on trading for a further twelve months. Each year, the Everyman paid off 10% of the debts to each creditor and each year every single creditor had to assent to the continuation of the moratorium – just one person refusing to agree would have meant the Everyman going into liquidation.[7]

Newman and the board seemed to be floundering and unsure of what to do next. They were deeply in debt, the theatre was dark and they had no actors, no shows and no Director of Productions. Thanks to the moratorium they were able to hobble on to the next crisis and again turned to Coventry for their salvation.

Ian Mullins, a seasoned rep man both as actor and director, was working at the Belgrade in late summer 1961, when he was invited to an interview for the post of Director of Productions at the Everyman. He recalls, 'It was not a very good interview and I am afraid I had the impression that the Everyman Board did not quite know what or who they were looking for. However, I was offered the job with John Ridley appointed as General Manager.'

This turned out to be the best and most far-reaching decisions the Board had ever made and Mullins' arrival at the Everyman was to

Clarkson Rose (left) and Pauline Allen in *Cinderella*, 1960
photo: Gerald Pates, Gloucester

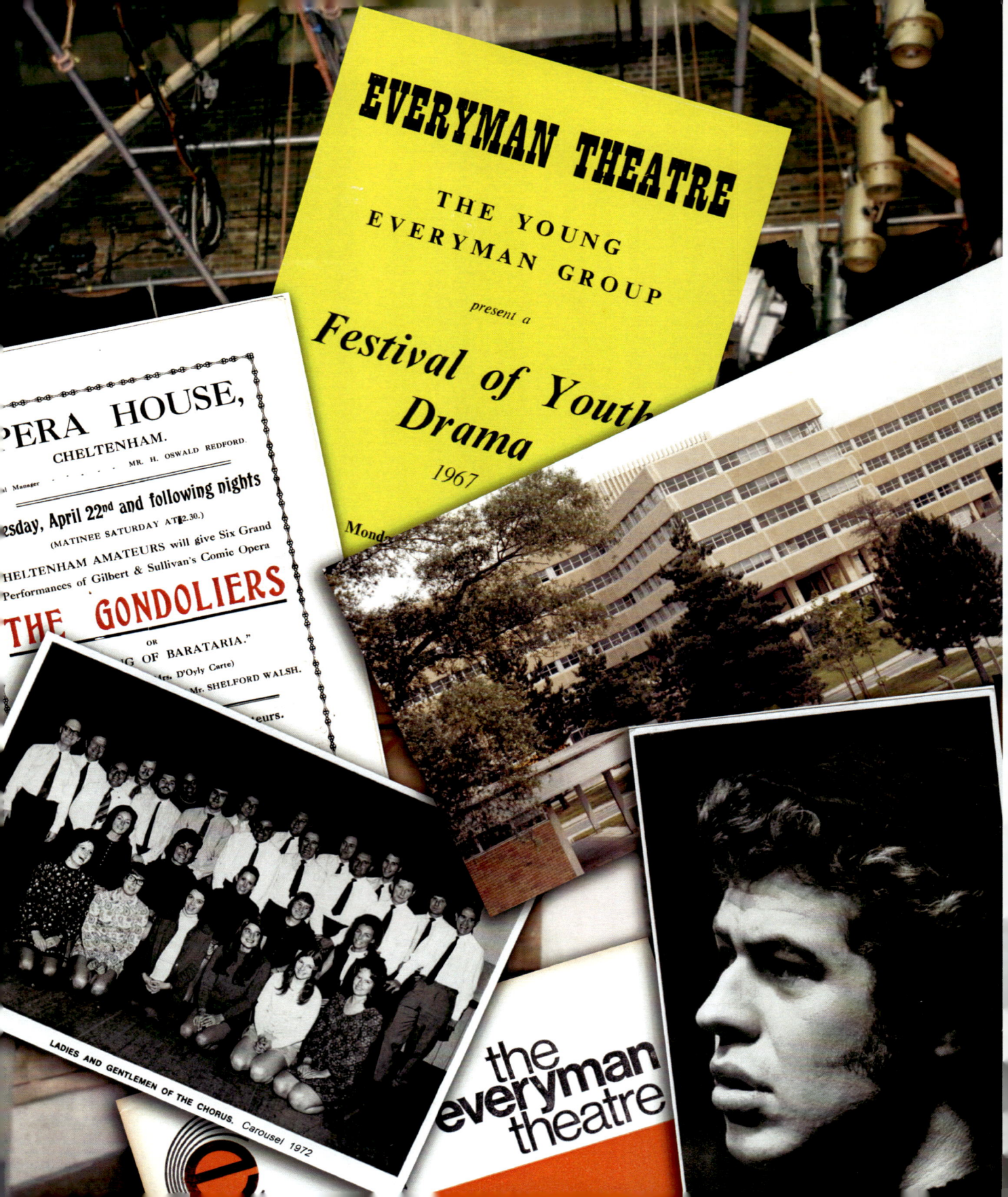

EVERYMAN THEATRE

THE YOUNG EVERYMAN GROUP

present a

Festival of Youth Drama

1967

Mond...

OPERA HOUSE, CHELTENHAM.

...l Manager .... MR. H. OSWALD REDFORD

...esday, April 22nd and following nights
(MATINEE SATURDAY AT 2.30.)

...HELTENHAM AMATEURS will give Six Grand
Performances of Gilbert & Sullivan's Comic Opera

THE GONDOLIERS
OR
...G OF BARATARIA."

...... Mrs. D'Oyly Carte)
...... Mr. SHELFORD WALSH.

LADIES AND GENTLEMEN OF THE CHORUS. Carousel 1972

the everyman theatre

Chapter 9

YEG, ETA, CODS & GCHQ
Lots of initial support

There is a strong case to support the proposition that without GCHQ there would be no Everyman Theatre. David Phillips, a Russian linguist worked at GCHQ as did his wife, Eunice. Phillips worked mainly training and teaching other Russian linguists and Roger Nicholls, Board member and Chairman of the Everyman Theatre Association, remembers him as being well suited to the task. 'David was a born school master. I don't know if he actually had taught, but the office had its fair share of ex-teachers who were recruited at Bletchley.' David Phillip's contribution to the survival of the theatre is acknowledged and commemorated with a plaque in the Everyman foyer.

Dudley Owen, who for ten years was the driving force behind the Everyman Board of Directors, was also a GCHQ man, as was Roger Nicholls. The three thousand employees at the establishment's two sites in Cheltenham, Benhall and Oakley, would provide a keen and loyal audience for over forty years.

GCHQ or Government Communications Headquarters to give it its full name, came to Cheltenham after the war. Until 1946 it had been known as the Government Code and Cypher School (GC&CS) and had been based at Bletchley Park, the wartime code braking establishment near Milton Keynes.

Most of GCHQ moved to Cheltenham in 1951, followed in 1969 by Communications-Electronics Security Department which then became CESG.

GCHQ Benhall. C Block in the mid 50s.
Crown Copyright. Reproduced by permission, Director, GCHQ

Roger Nicholls in 2010
Photo; Michael Hasted

Roger Nicholls came to Cheltenham in 1964 and it was through Dudley Owen that he became involved with the Everyman. 'Dudley Owen was one of the people who planned the move of GCHQ to Cheltenham. They went round assorted towns in England but it needed to be further than 'N' miles from London i.e. out of the range of any nuclear bomb dropped on the capital. They chose Cheltenham because it was ideally situated and in those days had good rail links; *The Cheltenham Flyer* train was still running then.

'But I think they just liked Cheltenham, it was respectable. The town was in a poor state at the time, rather shabby. A lot of outlying villages around the town which are now ridiculously expensive and trendy were occupied by GCHQ people. They bought houses for next to nothing and made a huge killing.

'It's true, if it hadn't been for GCHQ Cheltenham would have declined and the Everyman would probably never have got off the ground. There were so many people working at GCHQ that it was difficult to avoid them socially. I remember when I first came to Cheltenham I was told not to join anything because half the people you'll meet there will be from here. And that probably applied the ETA.'

Dudley Owen joined Bletchley Park in June 1940 and worked in Hut 8(RR) Records Research. In 1944/45 he was head of N.S. Signals Office in N.S.VII and moved to Cheltenham with GCHQ in the 1950s.

Without GCHQ Robert Whelan would never have joined the Young Everyman Group (known as the 'YEGs') and possibly would never have become an actor. Whelan's father, Ronald, had come to Cheltenham to work at GCHQ with his young family in 1953 after working in Hut 7, Block C at Bletchley Park during the war.

Whelan remembers his first impressions of the theatre. 'It was Christmas 1961, I was fifteen and still at the Grammar School. Towards the end of the autumn term, Pete Beard, who was in the 6th form and a couple of years older than me, told me about the Young Everyman Group. He said that he and some others had started the YEGs to help support the theatre by doing voluntary work and organizing fundraising activities. Was I interested? It was something you could put down on your university application. And you would meet girls. I was in.

'There was a sign above the door at the side of the theatre; it said Stage Door. I walked cautiously through a small entrance lobby. To the left was a phone booth under some stairs, then another door. To the left stone stairs rose up into the gloom. Straight ahead was a heavy steel fire door which led onto the stage. I went through and entered a strange and wonderful new world.'

At the public meeting at St. Mary's Hall in October 1959, which established the Cheltenham Theatre Association, one of the speakers was a young Nicholas Barter-Spencer, chairman of the Association's newly formed Young People's Committee. This later became, under Mr. Barter-Spencer's leadership, The Young Everyman Group. He explained the main task of his committee was to attract young people to the theatre saying, 'They deserve a voice in what is to be presented and we shall do everything to see that they have one'.[1]

From humble beginnings, just over two years later YEG membership had soared to 1,500.

Nicholas Barter-Spencer later dropped the Spencer and went on to have a distinguished career in the theatre as a director and, between 1993 and 2007, principal of Royal Academy of Dramatic Arts. His mother, actress Sylvia Barter, was a member of Ian Mullins' company in 1967.

It was a great thing to be a YEG in Cheltenham in the sixties. An annual subscription of five shillings (25p) enabled members to buy half-price tickets for the theatre during the week and for 1/9d (about eight pence) they could all pile into the Gallery on a Friday night and afterwards meet in the gods bar for a coffee and a chat with the cast. If they wanted, they could also go on the rota to help out backstage. It was the best club in town and Julian Slade was their president.

David Gilmore, a successful director who has worked at the National and whose production of *Grease* has been running in the West End for many years, had his first experience of the theatre thanks to the YEGs. 'I was in the 6th form at the Grammar School. I'd heard about the YEGs so I enrolled, in 1964 it must have been, I think I was seventeen. I ended up spending every spare minute there until three in the morning sometimes. I absolutely fell in love with it.

'I remember the very first night I went backstage. I turned up and, not knowing anything, walked through the pass door and found myself standing in the prompt corner in the middle of a show. There was blaze of golden light coming off the stage and the audience was

Left: The old fly floor

Right: The stage crew c.1965. Robert Whelan is fourth from the left.

roaring with laughter and off the stage, into the wings swept Josephine Tewson, dressed in a crinoline or whatever. She looked at me, smiled, turned round and went back on stage to a round of applause. I've never forgotten that moment. I had stepped into a golden and welcoming world. It's the smell I remember. A smell you don't get any more; size from the scene painting, make-up and dust. You tell people in the business now and they don't know what you are talking about.'

Ian Mullins remembers the importance of the keen young volunteers. 'God knows what we would have done without the YEGs. We were so understaffed to begin with because we had so little money. We had Noel Newman breathing down our necks the whole time and we were only able to do it because we'd been given £3,000 by the Council. Without the YEGs helping out backstage I don't know how we would have managed.'

In the mid-sixties the Association was in full swing. Sunday evening entertainment for members were frequently mounted in the theatre with the actors pleased to perform their party pieces. However, one idea that seemed to border a little on desperation was the creation of a baby-sitting scheme by the YEGs who offered to look after babies when the parents went to the theatre.

In September 1970, the ETA and the YEGs joined forces to create another ambitious scheme designed to make money: Theatre Week. The brochure said, 'Theatre Week is designed primarily as an expression of pride in our theatre and as such deserves all the encouragement you can give it'.

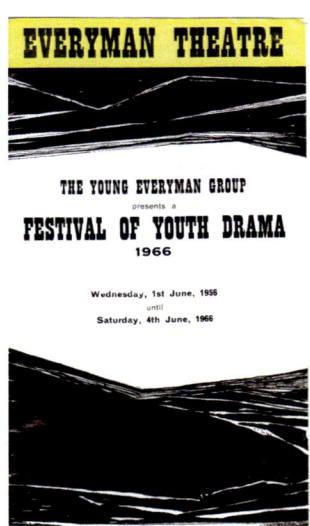

The annual conference of the Federation of Playgoers Associations was held in Cheltenham at the beginning of October 1966[2] to which groups similar to the ETA from all over the country sent representatives.

On the Sunday, Ian Mullins addressed the conference on the theme of *The Theatre in Cheltenham* which was followed by a grand luncheon at the Pittville Pump Room with guest speaker Lord Goodman, the then Chairman of the Arts Council. The event was also attended by Sir Donald Wolfit, President of the Association whose company had been frequent visitors to the old Opera House during and after the war.

The annual Festival of Youth Theatre, staged by the YEGs, was created in 1963. Its aim was to invite school theatre groups from the surrounding area to present a mixed and ambitious bag of plays for the week long festival. The programme was nothing if not ambitious and demanding. Some of the plays presented would have tested the most able rep company, but the schools were undaunted. From small beginnings it was to become, over the next decade and more, an important date in the theatre's programme.

Martin Johnson, Professor of Reproductive Sciences at Cambridge University was, while at Cheltenham Grammar School, one of the main recruiters for back-stage volunteers from the school and was chairman of the YEG in 1963. He said of the new Festival, 'For the first time in its history The Everyman is being occupied for a whole week by The Young Everyman Group, none of whom is older than

above left: A Friday night, after-show, YEG party in the Gallery coffee bar c.1962. Valentine Dyall chats to members

twenty-one. Not only are young people providing the staff for the week, they are also acting and bringing you six different plays with six different casts and sets. In fact, six local schools and colleges are entering a play each, one to be performed each night, beginning on Monday, 20th May.

'Probably the highlight of the week, and our most ambitious selection, is the first performance ever of *Les Enfantes Terribles* based on Jean Cocteau's superb novel. Already, one or two of the productions have been given very warm receptions by the press in pre-festival performances. I would like to close by asking all of you who regularly patronise the theatre to help us in our venture to make this drama festival a big success, indeed *A Week for Youth*'.

Rodney Harris, the Chairman of the YEG at the time explained how it worked. 'Eight plays are being presented, spread over the first three days. The Saturday performance will be a repeat of the best two performances, one of which will win the Cheltenham Chamber of Commerce Challenge Trophy.'

Stephen MacDonald, an associate director at the time, adjudicated at the 1967 Festival. 'Even though the task of choosing the best of anything is thankless and unenviable, it gave me the opportunity of taking part in a project which was valuable to the theatre as a whole. I was looking out for enthusiasm and honesty of intention as much as final achievement. Nobody finally achieves anything; and even for those who went staggering home under the weight of trophies, or whatever loot was awarded, it was not their particular success that was important, it was the existence of the Festival.'

In spite of the 1973 Festival being cancelled due to lack of entrants, in 1974 it was back with a vengeance. The programme demonstrated how confident they all were. First up was King's School, Worcester, whose drama group performed Arthur Miller's *A View From the Bridge*, Sir Thomas Rich from Gloucester came up with *Twelfth Night* while Evesham's Prince Henry School presented *Roots* by Arnold Wesker. On the Thursday Cheltenham's Pate's Grammar School put on Chekov's *Three Sisters* with a little help from some boys – at this time Pate's was just a girls' school.

The 1975 Festival was certainly no less ambitious. The adjudicator, Richard Carrington, who played the Vicar in *The Archers*, had the difficult task of judging a rich and varied collection of plays. They included *The Importance of Being Ernest*, Brendan Behan's *The Hostage* and Alan Bennett's *Forty Years On*. Nicholas Barter, who by now was a successful director, sent his good wishes to the theatre on its tenth anniversary. 'Many congratulations on such a splendidly successful first ten years. Since I was the first chairman of the YEG and also did my first professional job at the Everyman, the life of your theatre is of personal interest to me. I am particularly happy to see that the support of the young people for the theatre is so lively, and may you go from strength to strength in the next ten years.'

At the end of 1987 the Association's coffers needed topping up and it was decided to hold a *Gala Fund Raising Evening in Celebration of the Arts*. The event was hosted by John Doyle and had contributions by William Gaunt, who at that time was the Patron of the ETA, Stephanie Turner and Nicholas Smith.

Although a professional theatre, the Everyman plays host to the town's leading amateur companies. The Cheltenham Operatic and Dramatic Society (CODS) has a history even older than the theatre itself. It was founded in 1883 and has used the theatre on an annual basis almost since it first opened. CODS is Cheltenham's oldest theatrical society and produces two musicals and one play each year, together with the occasional concert. The summer musical is performed at the Everyman Theatre. The autumn play and the winter musical are staged at The Playhouse Theatre in Bath Road. In fact, the CODS were the very last show to appear on the stage of the old Opera House before it closed in 1959.

Numerous other amateur companies used the theatre, including performances by the Working Men's College in 1898 and 1899.

EVERYMAN THEATRE

THE SALAD DAYS

Tuesday, 26th December 1961

CHELTENHAM

Chapter 10

Hay Days and Salad Days
The future's bright, the future's yellow 1961-1971

There are those who consider the rep years, especially those between 1961 and 1983, to be the finest and most important in the theatre's long and varied history. 'I absolutely agree with that,' says Roger Nicholls. 'I couldn't believe the quality of the work being done there. I think the first thing I saw was *Tamburlaine the Great* in November 1964 with Harvey Ashby and Josephine Tewson. I'd been a regular theatre-goer in London and this was as good as anything I'd seen there.'

When the 32-year-old Ian Mullins and General Manager John Ridley, who had founded the Century Theatre in Keswick, took over the Everyman in the autumn of 1961, they created a company from scratch. Mullins brought with him new actors and a completely new backstage team. It was this new troupe that was to create the true foundation for repertory companies which were to provide shows for the theatre for the next thirty-five years.

Because of the precarious financial situation, the appointments of Mullins and Ridley were not set in stone. As late as September 1961 the future of the theatre was still hanging in the balance. In an article headed *Appointments Anticipate an Opening*, *The Stage* revealed that if a grant of £2,000 from the Cheltenham Council was not forthcoming, it was unlikely that the Everyman would re-open.[1] The Council eventually made a grant of £2,900 and, with the money in the bank, Mullins was free to get started.

l-r: John Ridley, Noel Newman, Valentine Dyall, Ian Mullins, Robert McBain, George Waring and Josephine Tewson seated c.1962

Ian Mullins' first production at the Everyman was *Meet Me By Moonlight* which opened on 7th November 1961 after the theatre had been closed for twenty weeks. By the time his second show, Robert Bolt's *A Man for All Seasons,* opened a couple of weeks later, the company that was to be the backbone of the rep for many years to come was already in place.

Josephine Tewson joined the fledgling company for the Bolt play at the beginning of November 1961 to play Sir Thomas More's wife, Alice. She has fond memories of Cheltenham. 'My time at the Everyman was one of the happiest I spent in rep. I loved the theatre when I first saw it and it's such a beautiful town with wonderful countryside around – not that we ever got time to see it.

'The rep was of a very high standard. I had worked with Ian and Helen [Dorwood, Ian Mullins' wife] at Salisbury but I didn't meet Bill Gaunt until Cheltenham. Ian directed the second play I was in,

The More the Merrier, just before Christmas. We were under a lot of pressure and I got the impression that if we hadn't built up the takings by the end of *Salad Days* the theatre may well have become part of Cavendish House.'

In addition to Josephine Tewson and William Gaunt, the actors Mullins brought together included Robert McBain, George Waring, Norman Jones, Roberta Maxwell, Lionel Thomson, David Kelsey, Ralph Nossek, Stephen Hancock, Helen Dorwood and Valentine Dyall.

Dyall had become famous as *The Man in Black* on radio between 1936 and 1955. In 1962 he played Canon Chasuble in *The Importance of Being Ernest* at the Everyman, a part his father, Franklyn Dyall, had created in the first production of the play in London in 1895. Dyall senior had often played the old Opera House, including an appearance in 1941 in *Napoleon Couldn't Do It*.

After the success of *Wildest Dreams* the year before, Ian Mullins was to choose another Slade/Reynolds musical, *Salad Days,* as his first Christmas show, in 1961. *Salad Days* was a bit of whimsical silliness ,even in the naive, easily pleased early fifties. It's about a couple of youngsters, just down from Oxbridge, who are given a piano to look after. It turns out the piano is magic and makes everybody dance. *Les Mis* it's not. Nevertheless, it is a show of great charm, some catchy tunes and the opportunity for some very funny scenes. Apart from holding the West End record it has been put on three times at the Everyman. The original magic piano is on view in the V&A Museum theatre collection next to one of Pete Townsend's smashed guitars.

Robert Whelan vividly recalls *Salad Days* and his first encounter with the backstage area of the Everyman. He was still a pupil at Cheltenham Grammar School whose fine Victorian Gothic buildings then stood in the High Street, only a few hundred yards away from Regent Street.

'I just remember standing there. To my right was the gaping void of the auditorium with its vacant, staring, empty seats disappearing into the gloom. The stage was lit by working lights, large bare light bulbs. I picked my way across the stage amidst the chaos absorbing the sights and sounds and the heavy dusty smell. Theatres don't smell like that now. It was the smell of size; the glue which was boiled up to prime the canvas flats and then added to the paint. It smelled so strong because it was boiled down cow hooves. There was also a lot of dust which came from the hemp ropes used for flying.'

William Gaunt was a regular member of the company for several years. 'Ian and I had met at Salisbury in 1960, I think it was, and when

Valentine Dyall in *Ross*, 1962

Anne Carr, Norman Jones, Ralph Nossek & Josephine Tewson (front) in *The More the Merrier*, 1961
photos: Gerald Pates, Gloucester

left: William Gaunt in *A Man for All Seasons*, 1961

right: David Kelsey, Robert McBain & Lionel Thomson in *Hooray for Daisy*, 1962
photos: Gerald Pates, Gloucester

he took over Cheltenham I spent quite a lot of time there. I wasn't in everything because by that time I had already started to work on television quite a bit.'

However, Gaunt was very much involved with and committed to the Everyman. In the autumn of 1962, he appeared in three extremely demanding roles back to back starting with the title role in *Billy Liar* which opened on 11th September. Terence Rattigan's *Ross* opened on 25th September with Gaunt playing T. E. Lawrence immediately followed, two weeks later, by Pinter's *The Caretaker* in which again, he played the very challenging role of Davies.

'I did those plays in an incredible period of six weeks playing the lead in each one. It was extraordinary. Very intensive work indeed, three enormous parts, playing one in the evening and rehearsing another during the day. In fact, it was during this time that the Cuban Missile Crisis took place, but Ian and I were working so hard we completely missed it. The world could have ended and we'd never have known why. It was very hard work, that little stint, but it was a most enjoyable period for me. But I enjoyed all the productions I did in Cheltenham and I played a series of marvellous parts.'

Despite Mullins' new broom approach, the backstage area of the theatre, which had hardly changed since the theatre was built seventy years earlier, was not touched and rarely swept.

There was no shower, only one lavatory backstage and three cramped dressing rooms. Jo Tewson remembers it well, 'The dressing rooms left an awful lot to be desired. You're used to being in terrible dressing rooms when you've been not that long in the business. But you expected it while working your way up through twice nightly. But it was absolutely lovely, smashing'.

There was no real Green Room for the actors to relax in either, but there was an area upstage by the dressing room stairs, opposite the quick change room, that served as a sitting/kitchen area. David Gilmore, who went on to become a leading West End director, remembers, 'One of the unique qualities of the Everyman, that I have never come across at any other theatre, but which I think should be *de rigueur*, was the situation of the Green Room. It was close enough to the stage not to require a Tannoy relay, where anyone offstage for a short time could wait or drink coffee while staying in intimate touch with the continuing performance'.

The theatre's technical equipment was fairly antiquated too. The stage lighting was controlled from a small platform eight feet above the prompt corner. The old Strand Electric board looked as though it belonged in a railway signal box rather than a theatre. It had six banks of eight levers, each of which controlled a circuit. It took several hands to operate the board and quite a few feet too. Not only was it cumbersome, but also extremely dangerous. Robert Whelan

left: Bernard Smith, Michael Pearce and Peter Laird (seated) in *Guilty Party*, 1963 (The chair was from the Ellenborough Hotel and is now in the home of Stephen Boswell)

right: Roberta Maxwell in *The More the Merrier*, 1961
photos: Gerald Pates, Gloucester

The Everyman, c. 1964

remembers, 'In heavy downpours water dripped through the roof on to the electrics. I once saw the lighting man blown backwards as sparks arced around the live levers'.

Ian Mullins recalls that old board too. 'I remember during *A Man for All Seasons* watching with horror the electrician, shod in wellington boots and wearing rubber gloves, working an electrics board which should have been lodged in a museum years before'. It was finally replaced in the summer of 1963 with a fine, state of the art 48 way L.C. board which was set up in the stage-left box in the auditorium.

David Gilmore started work at the Everyman at this time. 'I was a Student ASM on £2 a week, learning the ropes – literally in some cases. I did a couple of shows with Hywel Price, the stage carpenter, learning how to make the sets. I did a couple of shows with Anthony

Lancaster, the electrician, learning about the lights and how to work the board and a stint with the designer, Clarence Wilson.

'You were a student for 40 weeks, there was a formal Equity contract, and by the end of that you should have learnt most of what you needed to work back-stage. I then became a fully fledged ASM on £7.50 a week.'

Ian Mullins was not a great one for commissioning original drama but was quite keen on new musicals. Long-time members of the company, David Kelsey and his partner Lionel Thomson, wrote or adapted a couple of musicals for the Everyman. Kelsey became the leading man for the 1963/4 season and Thomson, as well as being a reliable supporting actor was also, along with Stephen Hancock, the in-house pianist.

Kelsey and Thomson wrote a musical called *Solo* for the company which opened the new season in July 1962. It was a sort of cross between *West Side Story* and *Coronation Street*. In fact, a then star of *Coronation Street*, Philip Lowrie, was brought in to play the lead. The story was all to do with motor bikes and did its best to be relevant and urban. The set was a representation of a fairground Wall of Death made from scaffolding. Robert Whelan has recollections of the building of it. 'Steve Collins was the assistant stage carpenter who had worked as a scaffolder and claimed that he could erect it. So, on the Sunday we built this scaffolding tower in the middle of the stage.

'We came in Monday morning to find that the it had walked down stage and was resting against the safety curtain. The old stage had a very steep rake, much more so than now. Without the iron it would have walked right into the stalls.'

The programme notes for *Solo* claimed, "It all happens around some industrial town or other, between this street and the next." Unfortunately though, it didn't really happen on stage. The company was rather out of its depth with such an ambitious project lacking, as it did, any good or real singers or dancers.

In spite of the relatively poor reception of *Solo*, Mullins commissioned David Kelsey to adapt the old *Maria Marten in the Red Barn* story for January 1963. This production was more successful because it was played as a Victorian melodrama which did not need the all-singing, all-dancing spectacle that *Solo* had failed to deliver.

The prompt corner just prior to demolition in 1983. The platform was orgininally the location of the old Strand lighting board. From 1963 it was used for the sound desk.

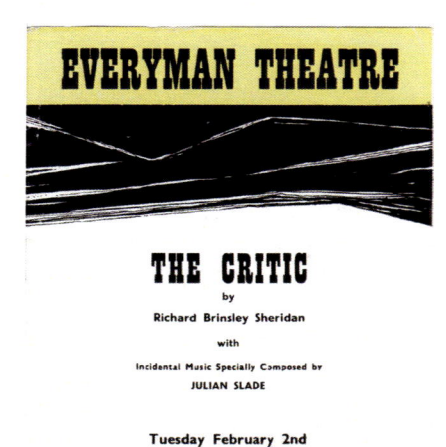

But not everything went according to plan when, during one performance, a potentially fatal accident occurred. David Gilmore was backstage at the time. 'I was in the flies for *Maria Marten* and Frank Middlemas was playing the murderer, William Corder. The final scene of the play is his execution for which there was a proper scaffold with a trap-door and a lever.

'The noose was put round his neck, the lever pulled and he fell through the trap. Of course, there was a wire attached to a harness he was wearing to take his weight. There was a resounding crack and the wooden batten to which the wire was attached broke and came swinging in towards us. Frank fell straight through the trap and finished up in a heap on the floor as the company sang the final song and the curtain came in. He was fine but there was a very nasty red mark around his neck.'

Despite the success of *Salad Days*, it was a couple of years before Julian Slade was to work with Mullins again. In March 1963, he set the songs in *As You Like It* to music and later that year, in October, his new musical *Nutmeg and Ginger,* written without Dorothy Reynolds, opened at the Everyman. The cast included John Warner who had created the part of Timothy in the original West End production of *Salad Days* in 1954.

By mid-1964, the success that Mullins had achieved at the Everyman was reflected in the choice of Council of Repertory Theatres to hold its conference in Cheltenham that year. The 72nd Conference and 22nd Annual General Meeting of C.O.R.T. was held at the Everyman on 25th June.[2]

At the end of 1964 Mullins decided to put on one very old play and one brand new one. To celebrate Christopher Marlowe's four hundredth anniversary, *Tamburlaine the Great*, which so impressed Roger Nicholls, opened on 3rd November. But David Gilmore, who carried a spear in the show, remembers thinking that perhaps Mullins had bitten off more than he could chew.

'With the exception of Tyrone Guthrie's 1951 production at the Old Vic starring Sir Donald Wolfit, this was the first professional production since 1588; an incredibly ambitious undertaking. The problem was that there was no one in the company who could take on the title role. Ian was getting desperate and bizarrely, at the very last minute put an advert in *The Stage* saying 'Wanted, Actor to play Tamburlaine'.

'The actor who finally did it was Harvey Ashby and at the same time a very young Robin Ellis joined the company straight from university for his first professional job.'

Dorothy Reynolds

The new play that November was written by a member of the company, David Monico. *Cabbages and Kings* was premiered at the Everyman on 24th, but not before overcoming a few hurdles of its own.

In those days, theatre was censored by the Lord Chamberlain and his famous blue pencil hovered like the sword of Damocles over all new writing. The text of every show had to be submitted to his office for approval before a license could be issued for its performance.

He had an issue with Monico's play and, on 5th November, less than three weeks before the play was to open, the assistant comptroller at St. James Palace wrote to John Ridley saying, 'I am desired by the Lord Chamberlain to write to you about the above named play. I am to inform you that the Lord Chamberlain cannot allow the dialogue given in the annexure to this letter and it must be altered or omitted altogether. In the latter case an undertaking must be given to that effect. Should it be your intention to substitute any dialogue, then the alteration must be submitted before it may be used'. The problem was on page 65 – the word 'fart'.

Despite the significant work done on the façade and front of house during the creation of the Everyman, not much was done to the auditorium and it began to look a little worse for wear. Luckily, there was someone in the building who was willing to take matters in to his own hands. When the theatre opened after its summer break in June 1965, many patrons would have perhaps got the impression that the auditorium had been redecorated. It had not, but a great deal of gilding of cherubs and other features had been carried out in addition to its receiving a thorough cleaning. The idea of gilding, or rather painting, the plasterwork came from Alan Black, one of the assistant stage managers, who carried out all this work himself during the summer recess. The auditorium got its almost as-good-as-new makeover for the cost of the paint – about £2.

Splendid and generous though Alan Black's efforts were, the professionals were finally called in two years later to carry out a more substantial makeover. The 1967 work was undertaken by local firm H.H. Martyn & Co. at a cost of less than £2000.

The company, who had undertaken a lot of maintenance and restoration work in the theatre over the years, were one of Cheltenham's greatest but least known enterprises. H.H. Martyn & Co. were originally monumental masons, established in 1888, occupying a site on the corner of College Road and the High Street. By 1905, the company employed about 200 people at its Sunningend Works located alongside the railway between Gloucester Road and Rowanfield Road. Over the years the company was to become one of the finest manufacturers of wooden, plaster, stone and cast metal monumental and decorative

Robert Whelan in *The Cherry Orchard*, 1965

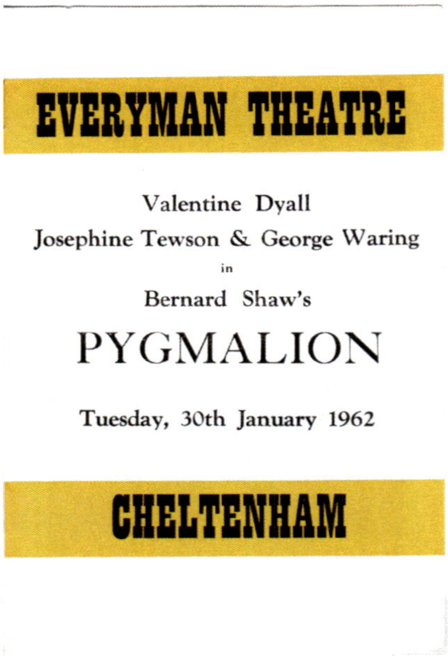

objects in the country. Among other commissions, it made the wood panelling on the *Titanic*, the Speaker's Chair in the House of Commons and the pulpit in St. Paul's Cathedral. Consequently, they were well suited and qualified to work on Cheltenham's theatre.

General Manager John Ridley left in April 1965 to work at the Malvern Festival Theatre and was replaced by Rae Hammond, a former magician, entertainer and civil servant. He remembered his first impressions of the theatre. 'On a snowy day in March 1965 I first saw the auditorium of the Everyman Theatre. It was this, rather than the extra £2 per week I was offered, that decided me to move there from the Birmingham Rep.'

Rae Hammond was an interesting man. He seems to have been a born entertainer who spent most of his life as a civil servant and the rest in theatre management. In 1946 he joined the Combined Services Entertainment and spent the next couple of years constantly touring the Far East, first of all with a variety unit and then in revues where fellow artists included Peter Nichols, Stanley Baxter, Kenneth Williams, John Schlesinger and Reg Varney.

The company was the inspiration for the hit 1970s television sitcom *It Ain't Half Hot Mum* and the magician character in Peter Nichols play *Privates on Parade* was based on Hammond. *Privates* won the 1977 Laurence Olivier Award for Best New Comedy.

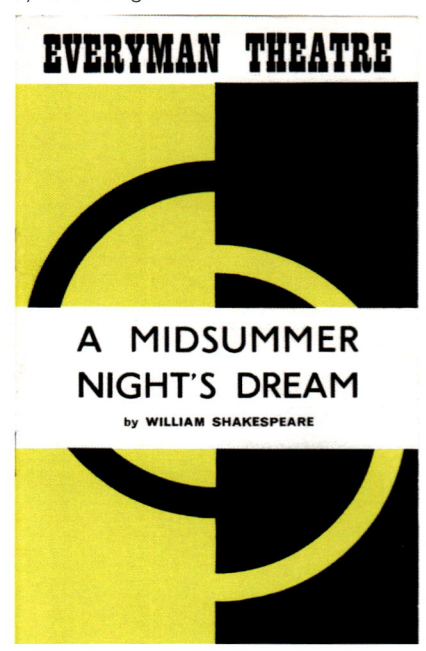

After five years in charge, Mullins decided it was time for a few changes. In 1966 it was decided the Everyman needed a new programme design and *The Echo* organised a competition. It was won by 17-year-old art student Richard Bryant, but Samantha Hodges' father also entered. 'My dad, Peter Hodges, who was 24 at the time and working as a salesman at Drakes, in the furniture department, entered a competition to design a programme for the Everyman. His design came second and was used by the theatre for all of the 1968/9 season.'

In the summer of 1967, a 27-year-old Penelope Keith joined the company. She had already worked in rep around the country and had had a couple of stints with the Royal Shakespeare Company. Her first part was Madame Arcati in Noël Coward's *Blithe Spirit*, a role with which she returned to the Everyman as a big star in 2004 prior to a successful West End run. She went on to play Mrs. Sullen in *The Beaux' Stratagem* in September 1967 and in October she played Goneril in Ian Mullins' production of *King Lear*. In November she played Olga in Barry Justice's production of Chekov's *The Three Sisters*.

In spite of changes made by Mullins, including an experiment with three-weekly rep, there had been a dramatic fall in attendances with

below: The new programme design by Peter Hodge in 1966

The front of the theatre after it had been re-modelled as The Everyman c. 1960
Photo: Gloucestershire Echo

the result that in November 1967 Ian Mullins was dismissed. William Gaunt remembers the circumstances. 'He had started out doing marvellously, the theatre was really on the map and he had built it up after David Giles' unsuccessful period. Ian and Helen were really settled in; they'd bought a house up on Cleeve Hill and he certainly wanted to stay on.

'By that time Ian had been there for six or seven years and the Board were just looking for a change. I think one of the reasons they wanted someone new is because Ian was very much a traditionalist. He believed basically in what he'd learned from Reggie Salberg at Salisbury, that you should give the audience what they wanted and throw in the odd classic or musical. A lot of reps since then failed because they did a lot of gloom and doom modern things which provincial audiences didn't want.'

The decision to get rid of Mullins was by no means unanimous and caused a rift behind the scenes, as Roger Nicholls recalls. 'The Board

THE BACKSTAGE AREA PRE 1983

left: The grid. The wheel that raised and lowered the paint frame

right: The gas ring used to boil up the size to mix the scene paint   *Photo by Edward Bottle*

and the Association had a big row at one point on the dismissal, or rather lack of re-appointment of Ian Mullins. The Board and the ETA at that time were so intertwined that Noel Newman was chairman of both. The original ETA, in effect, became the board in 1960. I remember the publicity when the Board decided it wasn't going to renew Ian's contract. The ETA didn't like this and broke away and elected its own chairman.'

The Stage, in an article headed *Mullins Mystery Shock Sacking* covered the story in some detail. After announcing the Board's verdict, Noel Newman decreed that there should be no discussion of the decision in his presence. However, the Board did want to discuss it and another meeting was set up to consider the sacking. At this point, Newman left the meeting and resigned his position as Chairman of the ETA.

According to *The Stage*, the resident company was extremely disturbed by the decision and felt the reasons should be made public. They felt the sacking implied criticism of the work done at the theatre and, by association, themselves. Mullins is quoted in the article as saying, 'The theatre is now firmly established and the time is now ripe to

THE BACKSTAGE AREA PRE 1983

left: The prompt corner

right: The tiny basin, the only source of water on the paint frame
Photos by Edward Bottle

develop it to its full potential. Having come this far with the company, I naturally want to see the job through'.

Newman continued to give no reason for Mullins' sacking. Stephen MacDonald, the company's leading man, demanded a public meeting for both the actors and public to air their grievances and to receive a satisfactory answer from the Board. The meeting was arranged to take place in the theatre on 10th December but at the last moment permission was withdrawn and the Town Hall was used instead.

The protest did force the Board's hand and they were finally obliged to break their silence. The reasons they gave for Mullins' sacking was that he was 'inexperienced and ineffective in the commercial and financial field and unable to reconcile his artistic ambitions with the necessity for a realistic budget'. Mullins replied that if that had been the case the theatre would have closed some time ago.[3]

Malcolm Farquhar, who took over the theatre a couple of years later, has an opinion as to why Mullins was sacked. 'He was too good. The Arts Council were the villains of the piece. I wished I could have

The old stairs to the dressing rooms just before demolition in 1983. The kitchen/Green Room was just to the left.

blown them to smithereens at times. They had a policy, they used to get people like Ian and me and put them into fledgling theatres and when we had succeeded and got the box office up they would get someone else in. Ian had a tough time here.'

David Gilmore sympathises. 'Running any rep is knackering – you're reading plays, you're casting plays, you're directing plays and you're attending board meetings. It is a knackering job. But when I look back, thinking what Ian did at the Everyman, it was like running a mini National Theatre. The programming he did was incredible. I think it was absolutely a beacon of how to run a repertory theatre.' But nevertheless, Ian Mullins' days as Director of Productions at the Everyman were over and Michael Ashton took over.

Michael Ashton has his own view and said of Mullins demise, 'I know that Ian Mullins had really been there too long. I don't want to be unkind about it, but he had been there a very long time as had some of the actors. The whole thing had got terribly tired and needed shaking up. I suspect that The Arts Council got onto the board and said they needed a change. I'm pretty sure that's what happened. The job was advertised and the Arts Council rang me up and asked me to apply because they'd seen some stuff of mine at Colchester which they liked and I got the job'.

1968 saw the start of a long relationship between the Everyman and the Cheltenham Literature Festival. Following continuing complaints about the acoustics at the Town Hall, it was decided to hold the whole of the Festival at the theatre. Three out of the six evenings were staged events, including Michael MacLiammoir's one-man show, *The Importance of Being Oscar*. However, what the theatre gained in intimacy and good acoustics it lost in available space. One of the casualties of the cramped conditions was the popular book exhibition. The following year the Festival returned to its spiritual home, the Town Hall.

It was about this time that Theatre in Education was beginning to become an important part of the theatre's brief. The department was run by Roland Metcalf, who had previously been technical director at the Everyman. He was assisted by actors from the company: Pamela Scotcher, David Sands, James Hogan and Peter Gregory.

In his programme notes for 22nd October 1968 Ashton wrote, 'During the run of *Loot* we are hosts, on the 25th October, to delegates from the British Medical Association's Annual Conference which is being held in Cheltenham. It has been a source of great satisfaction to us to have been fully booked for this performance for nearly eighteen months – in fact, from long before we even knew what play was on. We hope that the BMA enjoys their evening with us'.

Unfortunately, the doctors did not enjoy the show at all. They were, according to complaints received by Noel Newman, 'appalled and disgusted'. 'I didn't direct *Loot*,' explained Ashton in 2010, 'but whoever it was, did not do it very well and there were great dramas over it'. In fact the play is credited as being directed by Edmund Grey, assisted by Michael Ashton.

Ashton was carpeted at the Board meeting soon after. 'Noel thundered I was never, *never*, to present such a play again.' said Ashton. 'The Board then asked me what I was planning to produce next. I said I wasn't sure they would approve. It was a play about adultery and crime in London high society and was written by a convicted homosexual. 'No!' shouted Noel, but Dudley Owen, who was much quicker on the uptake, realised I was referring to *Lady Windermere's Fan*'.

There were rumours of another financial crisis in September 1969. Ashton said at the time, 'Let me emphasise that the theatre is *not* broke. We have modest reserves in addition to the small profit from last season. However, the continued heat wave has seen to it that we, along with many other theatres, have taken less money at the box office than we could reasonably have expected. I do not wish to encroach on our reserve funds. There's always the chance of a bad winter'.[4]

And it certainly turned out to be a bad one for Ashton. 'I don't like to talk about it, but my wife left me for a member of the company.' As a result of the collapse of his marriage, Ashton suffered what was described as 'a breakdown' and took some weeks off work. During his absence, the reins were once again taken up by Rae Hammond who brought in guest directors.

Ashton returned at the beginning of 1970 but his heart was no longer in it. 'When I came back, I simply didn't want to be there and everybody knew it. I was unhappy, I'd had a bad time but it was purely personal.' He was never to achieve the same success as Ian Mullins and continuing poor audiences sealed his fate. He didn't stay very long after coming back from sick leave and left six months before the completion of his contract. 'My reasons for leaving were completely personal,' he said in 2010, although a statement at the time said he was leaving 'to devote his time to writing and freelance work'.[5] His last show was *Wildest Dreams* in October 1970.

When Noel Newman, long standing Chairman of the Board of Directors, died in 1970, he was replaced by Edward Bradby who was principal of St. Paul's teacher training college in Cheltenham. Fellow director Dudley Owen, who had effectively been running the theatre since The Everyman was founded, also resigned from the board after retiring from GCHQ and was replaced by another GCHQ man, Roger Nicholls.

Michael Ashton

22 July - 8 August
Confusions
Alan Ayckbourn

4 - 27 November 1982
ROAR LIKE A DOVE
by Lesley Storm

CYRIL FLETCHER and **BETTY ASTELL** at their Sussex
Jolly and Henry as puppies.

GODSPELL
H. M. TENNENT LTD. by arrangement with EDGAR LANSBURY/ and CAMERON MACKINTOSH

SILVER JUBIL

EVERYMAN THEATRE
Evening 7.45
11 Dec. 73
Stalls
K 14
60p Inc. V.A.T.
TO BE RETAINED

Direction by JOE DAVIS
Setting by IAN DOW
conceived by JOHN-MICHAEL TEBELAK
SCHWARTZ

THE NATIONAL PRO
OF THE GREAT

Chapter 11

Purple Haze
The Malcolm Farquhar years 1971-1983

The swift departure of Michael Ashton left the Everyman in rather a vacuum. One couldn't just pick up the phone and get a new Director of Productions in at short notice. Luckily, a solution was close at hand, as William Gaunt explained. 'After Michael Ashton left and before Malcolm Farquhar took over, Rae Hammond was running the place. I did *Look Back in Anger* which George Waring, another member of the Ian's original company, directed.'

But around Christmas 1970 the Everyman was again in financial trouble. John Hurt, who had given up his job in banking to do public relations for Cyril Fletcher's forthcoming pantomime, heard alarm bells ringing. 'Cyril told me he thought there was a risk that the repertory theatre may close before *Dick Whittington* opened but that I should not worry as he would honour my contract.' According to Hurt, it was only the advance bookings for the panto that kept the theatre going.

In programme notes on 9th February 1971 Hammond explained his situation. 'As patrons will know, a new Artistic Director will shortly be appointed for the theatre, and he will take up his duties in time for the beginning of next season. Meanwhile, till the end of the present season, I am holding the fort here and I hope that in the programme of plays which I have chosen there will be something for everyone.'

Rae Hammond ran the theatre for six shows and managed to maintain a very high standard by a choice of popular, yet quality plays and

Rosamond Burne as Miss Prism and Richard Simpson as Canon Chasuble in *The Importance of Being Ernest*, 1971
photo: Gerald Pates, Gloucester

bringing in good directors. According to an article in *The Stage*, the Everyman, during that period, played to 73% of capacity and for two weeks, 85%.[1]

In fact, Malcolm Farquhar was one of the guest directors Hammond brought in, only a few weeks before he took on the job of Artistic Director. 'I came down as a guest director for Rae and did *Mansfield Park* in March 1971 at which time my appointment as new Director of Productions was confirmed.'

Malcolm Farquhar took up his new post as Artistic Director in May. 'I think I got the job on Rae and Margaret Davies' recommendation. I had worked in the Everyman rather a lot as an actor and director over the previous ten years so they knew my work. I had just directed five successful West End shows back to back and that impressed the Board enormously. I did come with a bit of prestige, I have to admit'.

But he had been left a difficult legacy by the previous incumbent. 'I thought Michael Ashton was a good director, but he couldn't do the business side. Towards the end of his time there, after he'd come back after his breakdown, the audiences went down to practically nil. I remember when I took over Rae Hammond said to me that I had an enormous task ahead of me because they were barely keeping afloat and the last production had taken only £250.

'My first show was *The Importance of Being Ernest,* which can usually be guaranteed to fill a theatre, but my second show was a disaster. The audiences didn't really trust anything that was going on there. It took me a whole season to get things back to a normal level.'

Farquhar's approach to running a rep theatre was not a million miles from that employed by Ian Mullins. Farquhar agreed. 'We both knew how to balance a box office. That was the most essential thing to do. Whenever anybody moaned at me because I was doing an Agatha Christie I would say, yes we are, because we lost money on the T.S. Elliot. After twenty years experience in rep I knew a hell of a lot of plays. I knew which would go, which could be revived and which ones couldn't.'

New, imaginative and innovative directors were not difficult to find, nor were competent accountants and bookkeepers. The problem for any provincial rep company was finding people who were both. Malcolm Farquhar had the edge on most of them. 'I was in *Salad Days* in 1961 at the Vaudeville Theatre in London and got very pally with Jack Gatti who owned the theatre. He taught me everything about running a theatre'.

Farquhar certainly brought a bit of colour to the theatre – purple. Roger Hendry, who had worked backstage since the late sixties, remembers his obsession with the colour. 'We even had a purple set at one point. Malcolm always dressed in purple and even had a purple moped with a purple crash helmet. It was one of those old fashioned ones like an upturned pudding basin with a leather chin strap. It was hysterical. He always used to have something on the set that was purple.'

One of the theatre's most interesting initiatives happened very soon after Farquhar took over – Action Theatre. Using the theatre on Monday nights when it was normally closed, Farquhar and members of the company put on experimental work. There was only ever one performance but it was a great success until Equity started making unrealistic stipulations and they had to end it.

As was necessary for anyone who worked in rep, Farquhar was often on the scrounge. By July 1971, he was already asking members of the audience to bring in any old clothes they didn't want in order to augment the theatre's wardrobe. Some years later he was to receive an offer from an unexpected source. 'In my final season I did *Dangerous*

Rosemary Leach in the premiere of *The Little Photographer* by Derek Hoddinott 1978
photo: Gerald Pates, Gloucester

Designer Donald Crosby at work in his studio c. 1975

Corner and Princess Anne came with her husband Mark Phillips. After the show she met all the actors and was very impressed with the costumes and asked where we got them. I explained that people often gave them to us and she said, 'Oh, I must ask Gran if she's got anything she doesn't want'.

Like any good manager, Farquhar had a great respect for the people he employed. 'Most of the success I had I can put down to the people I had around me. Carol Evans and Monica Heath were both brilliant stage-managers and Rae was behind me. Joan Wade was a lovely secretary, John Hurt, who was now working for the Everyman, did the publicity which was beautifully done. My designer, Donald Patel, who later changed his name to Crosby, was incredible.

'Our normal budget for the set was £600 though Donald would sometimes ask for another £100, but he would usually manage. He was such a beautiful painter, he could do anything. His sets were the talk of the town, some would get a round of applause when the curtain went up and the audience wouldn't stop applauding; you couldn't get on with the play. Donald could work miracles, he loved his work.'

Crosby remembers how he came to be working at the Everyman. 'The set I'd done for *Hedda Gabler*, in Canterbury, which Cleo Laine was in, was a sort of blackcurrant colour. Now Malcolm loved purple. Everything had to be purple and he obviously liked my set and offered me Cheltenham. His flat in Brighton was all purple and he insisted that there should be something purple on every set we did. He'd go looking for it if it wasn't immediately obvious.'

Farquhar's experience having worked in the West End such a lot meant he could call on the big names to come down to Cheltenham for a play.

'I brought down Peggy Mount and Cicely Courtneidge, Rosemary Leach, people like these. The problem was that the most I could pay was £40 a week so I would tempt them with plays I knew they wanted to do and I said that if they were successful I'd give them ten per cent of the box office. Of course, the audiences came flooding back to see these names. It took me about three years before we were getting regular full houses'.

Peggy Mount in The Anniversary, *1975 with David Harvey, Leslie Rhodes and Walter Kennedy*
photo: Gerald Pates, Gloucester

During Farquhar's first year the situation at the Everyman had greatly improved. The Accounts Report for 1972/73 showed audiences had increased from 108,000 in 1971 to over 134,000 in 1973. Box office revenues had also increased by £12,353 to a record £53,976.[2]

The pantomime for Christmas 1975 was *Babes in the Wood* starring Donald Hewlett and Michael Knowles, the bumbling officers double act from the wonderful BBC sitcom *It Ain't Half Hot Mum*. Rae Hammond must have had a wry smile on his face.

Although Farquhar's first year at the Everyman was a great success, the beginning of 1972 brought an unusual challenge. Malevolent external forces that were to bring many businesses, and almost the country itself to their knees, raised their ugly heads.

The infamous Three-Day Week was one of several measures introduced by Edward Heath's Tory Government to conserve electricity, the production of which was severely limited due to industrial action by coal miners. The effect was that from 1st January until 7th March 1972 commercial users of electricity would be limited to three specified consecutive days' consumption each week.

Mark Wynter and Tony Britton in *Sleuth*, 1977
photo: Gerald Pates, Gloucester

All over the country, businesses hung on by the skin of their teeth. The cinemas and many of the restaurants in Cheltenham were often forced to close but the Everyman was made of sterner stuff and managed to stay open during the ten week period. John Hurt explained how. 'I negotiated with a local fairground operator and we hired a generator from him. It was parked outside and fairground lights were erected throughout the auditorium and stage areas. When the power cuts came, the generator kicked in – we never missed a show ... and of course, the publicity value was immense. One of the plays affected was *A Streetcar Named Desire* starring Rosemary Leach.'

Josephine Tewson returned to the Everyman in 1975 in the unfamiliar role of director. 'I had already worked with Malcolm, we did *Free as Air* together in the West End' she recalls. 'I directed Alan Bennett's

Habeas Corpus. I had been in it in London and Malcolm was going to take one of the leading parts when we did it at Cheltenham and felt he couldn't direct as well, so he asked me. I had already directed a couple of plays for Ian Mullins at Basingstoke, so I wasn't a complete novice. I enjoyed directing. Looking back, I think I probably could have done more but being a bit lazy I didn't go out ferreting for that work. I would have been quite a hard task master. I really do not suffer fools gladly and as a director you have to be able to cajole and flatter and be very diplomatic.'

Mark Wynter, who had been a chart topping pop singer in pre-Beatles 1960s, became a successful actor and made many visits to the Everyman. 'I've been to Cheltenham, many, many times. I was there years and years ago when I was as a pop singer in about 1961. The first time I came as an actor was to the Everyman when it was run by Malcolm Farquhar and I was in *Sleuth* with Tony Britton. It was during that really hot summer of 1976. It was wonderful; I so enjoyed doing the play and working in the theatre.'

By July 1977 the Board of Directors had a new chairman when Christopher Powell took over from William Poeton and, at the end of 1978, Captain Mark Phillips became patron of the Everyman.

Peter Denyer started what was to be a long association with the Everyman in July 1978 soon after he had set up home in Cheltenham. He was already well known for his portrayal of the dim-witted Dennis Dunstable in the highly successful 1970s sitcoms *Please Sir* and its sequel, *The Fenn Street Gang*. His first play in the Everyman was *Double Edge* directed by Farquhar's assistant, Michael Napier Brown.

Another actor who was to achieve success on the small screen arrived at the Everyman in 1980. Tony O'Callaghan, later to find fame as Sergeant Matt Boyden during a twelve year stint in *The Bill*, started his career at the Everyman as an ASM. He recalls being very impressed on his first day at work. 'My first job was in Cheltenham. I remember getting to the theatre first thing in the morning before anyone else had turned up and just the cleaning people were there. Cheltenham is such a beautiful theatre. I remember walking onto the stage and the house lights were on and it was just wonderful. I thought 'Ahhh, this is it, I've arrived."[3]

The first production of 1981 was *Boeing-Boeing* which saw the welcome return, after thirteen years, of Ian Mullins and a further visit from Josephine Tewson. Mullins had for some time been running New Zealand's National Theatre, the Mercury, in Auckland. In April that year he also directed Arthur Miller's *The Price* in which both members of the resident directorial staff, Farquhar and Napier Brown appeared.

To coincide with Mullins' return, Rae Hammond paid tribute to his former boss by revealing his part in getting the theatre out of debt twenty years earlier. 'We owed well over £14,000 and we must forever remain grateful to our creditors for their patience and understanding for allowing a moratorium. By 1967, they had all been repaid. That this was achieved was partly due to the Arts Council who gave us special grants, but mainly due to Ian Mullins' skill in choosing suitable programmes and good casts. By the time he left, the £14,000 deficit had turned into a £5,000 surplus.'[4]

At about the same time, it became clear that another era at the Everyman was coming to an end and that another of its trustee stalwarts was getting a raw deal. On 30th April 1981, Rae Hammond placed a very curt advertisement in *The Stage* announcing he was resigning from his post on 30th June. The advert did not give any reason but the fact is, there had been a dispute over his salary and Hammond believed, that after all his years of service, he was being treated very badly. He had been General Manager for fourteen years and had provided the backbone to the theatre during the reign of three artistic directors. Malcolm Farquhar has very fond memories of him. 'His interest in the theatre was so great that if you mentioned any theatre he would be able to give the dimensions of the stage or whatever. Anything about a theatre, he'd know.'

Rae Hammond was a professional to his fingertips and was loved and respected by one and all – except perhaps Michael Ashton. 'Everybody loved him, I'm not sure they respected him. He could be a complete pain. He was mad about the theatre and the building and the chandelier and all that, but any money you spent on a show he resented bitterly. You can't do this, you can't have any money for that. He was endlessly asking me for budgets for shows that I was going to be doing six months ahead. He was money, money, money. To be fair, that was his job. He got on very well with Dudley Owen.

'Rae had no other life, he was quite extraordinary. No family that anyone knew about, no close friends, certainly no partner of any kind. He was very much a loner.'

Rae Hammond died as a result of a stroke on 22nd September 1995. He left instructions that there should be no ceremony when he died and he was buried without service or a funeral. He was replaced by John Hurt who had been the Public Relations Officer. He remembers that, 'Rae had his demons, a few more than most of the rest of us, I hope. He could be difficult to work with but he could also be charming and remained a friend until his death'.

The last production before the theatre closed for rebuilding in February 1983 was a new comedy, *Beside the Sea* by Brian Jefferies. It had first been announced that Eileen Page would star alongside Malcolm Farquhar but when she pulled out, her place was taken by another old favourite from Ian Mullins' 1960s company, Helen Dorwood.

The closure of the theatre for the £2m redevelopment was announced in mid-1982 with the possibility of as many as fifty redundancies. A spokesman said that hopefully some would be re-employed when the theatre re-opened two years later. Others would be offered other jobs with the council. There was also talk of continuing the rep at another venue in town but the Arts Council advised against this, fearing a fall in standards.[5] However, the closure did not stop some company diehards presenting pantomimes at the Town Hall.

Tony McEwan, Lee Fox and John Warner in *Hadrian the Seventh*, 1971
photo: Gerald Pates, Gloucester

The last performance took place on 26th February and a few weeks later, ninety-two years worth of history which was embedded in the fabric and patina of the backstage area was unceremoniously demolished. A couple of years later, before the theatre re-opened, Malcolm Farquhar would suffer a fate as ignominious as that of the theatre, never to return.

Josephine Tewson recalls, 'I was aware of the problems Malcolm had. I was in *Cider With Rosie* with Stephen Hancock which had been such a success that we were told that the theatre would re-open with it after the rebuilding. Next thing you know is that they'd sacked him and there was someone completely new. They treated him very badly. I blame the board, I really do. The problem with boards of directors, and it's not just Cheltenham, is that they are usually business men or whatever and they don't really know anything about theatre. I know both Ian and Malcolm had a long series of battles. But as an actor you are not always aware of this at the time. The director's job is to keep everybody happy so he's not going to foist his worries onto the company'.

THE GLOUCESTERSHIRE Everyman Theatre COMPANY LIMITED

3-26 February 1983

MALCOLM FARQUHAR
HELEN DORWARD
AND THE EVERYMAN COMPANY

in Brian Jefferies'

Beside the Sea

OUR FINAL PRODUCTION PRIOR TO CLOSURE for building improvement programme. Grand Re-opening—late 1984

Directed by
ANN STUTFIELD

Designed by
DONALD CROSBY

Season sponsored by
Cruden Developments Ltd.

William Gaunt was sad and surprised to see Farquhar go and rated him very highly. 'Malcolm was very successful. He was a very good theatre man, tremendous continuity and had very good companies.' Farquhar's fall from grace at the Everyman was to be a protracted and messy business.

Christopher Powell, who was the Chairman of the Board in 1983 when the theatre closed, told the company that the Arts Council would not retain anyone. But he announced that it had been arranged that they would all be asked back when the theatre re-opened, but that they should find jobs in the meanwhile. Malcolm Farquhar was not convinced. 'Sometime later I was taken aside by a friend of mine who was on the board who said it was a pity I didn't jack it all in because it was all getting so political and that things were not going as he thought they would.

'I got hold of Powell one day and said to him, 'If we're not coming back, people should be told, so they can get other jobs'. But he said, 'No, no, everything's fine and not to worry'. But, I later discovered, it had all been tied up, that the Arts Council had told them that if they didn't get a new Artistic Director the funding would cease.'

Nevertheless the Board was still, according to Farquhar, behaving as if he was coming back and asked him to plan the new season. 'David Phillips had gone to Powell and asked if he'd warned me about how things were going but Powell had said there was no need.'

Donald Crosby, like most other people, believed they would all be taken back. 'The understanding was that most of us would come back when the theatre re-opened, so much so that the town Council offered us work for three years to tide us over. I was offered work as a decorator painting council houses. But I had a friend, who was the theatre doctor at the time, who offered me work painting his house in Prestbury.

'I did lots of odd jobs. I cleaned the theatre offices for twelve hours a week. For those three years I lived as a pauper really just ticking over until we went back. Worst thing I ever did, of course, because at the end of three years we were told Malcolm wouldn't be coming back. Only a few of us returned; myself, Carol Evans, Roger Hendry and John Hurt.'

About six months before the theatre was due to re-open, a local magazine announced, 'One thing is certain, Malcolm Farquhar is not coming back to the Everyman'. Farquhar confronted the Board. 'They still denied it. Powell said he didn't know anything about it but then he came to me and said, 'there's been a certain alteration but it's only a technical thing'. He said I'd have to re-apply for the job but that I

The Everyman in 1982

would get it automatically. Well, that was the red light. Anyway, I was interviewed by the Board but I could see from their faces; they weren't making eye contact, I could see it was over.

'The only person who showed any remorse was David Phillips. After the Board had voted me out he phoned me and said he was so ashamed, he had resigned. It was not that they had not selected me but the way in which they'd done it.

'There were many aspects to the circumstances but the one thing I could not forgive was Powell not telling me. Myself and several of my staff wasted two years waiting around for something that was never going to happen. Donald Crosby was the only person who stayed but he deeply regretted it and left after eighteen months unhappy over what he considered to be the extravagance of the new regime.'

Malcolm Farquhar's departure had been unceremonious and equally sad. 'Powell refused to give me a reference and the ETA did not give me the usual farewell dinner. I was out.' Although he continued living in Cheltenham for many years, he had no more contact with the theatre.

But possibly the fact that Farquhar had been at the theatre for eleven years contributed to his demise and that it was perhaps a case of familiarity breeding contempt. It was perceived that he had, like Ian Mullins, just been around too long. Although he had worked

Malcolm Farquhar outside
the Everyman, October 2010
photo: Michael Hasted

elsewhere as an actor and director during the closure, he had never sought to leave Cheltenham for any other theatre and maybe, after eleven years at the Everyman, his drive, ambition and originality were not what they had once been. He said himself, 'I had done it all by then. If you are approaching sixty you're not going to be bouncing around anyone for tennis in weekly rep are you? And I didn't want to run another theatre'.

But by that time the winds of change were already blowing along Regent Street. Throughout the country, rep wasn't what it had been and the Arts Council seemed more interested in appointing administrators than Artistic Directors.

In the early eighties the Arts Council presented *The Glory of the Garden*, a policy document which proposed new and far-reaching changes for regional theatre in Great Britain. The changes would affect not only Cheltenham but repertory theatres all over the country.

Roger Hendry has witnessed many strange things in the theatre.
Photo 2010 by Michael Hasted

Chapter 12

Things that go bump in the night…
Spooky things and strange phenomena

Theatres are funny places. Often funny ha-ha and very often funny peculiar. One of the funny peculiar aspects is that most theatres, certainly old theatres, seem to be haunted. The Everyman is no exception. In fact, it seems, if all the stories are to be believed, to be more haunted than most.

Stately homes will certainly be top of the list for sightings of eerie apparitions but theatres will probably come in a very close second. The two have quite a lot in common which possibly accounts for their unwanted guests. Both theatres and country houses tend to have lots of dark, dusty corners and corridors. Both will have played host, over the years, to a multitude of colourful and eccentric characters and both will have lots of mysterious and intriguing stories to tell.

At the Everyman even John Ridley, who was a rather staid, tweed-jacketed gentleman, claimed to have seen the 'grey lady' sitting in the stage-right box.

Josephine Tewson tells the story of a strange experience that Lionel Thomson had while alone in the theatre one night. 'We had all finished the play and gone home and Lionel, who was musical director for the next show, had some work to do on the score. So he stayed behind, locked himself in – there was no stage door keeper in those days – and was sitting at the piano in the pit.

The haunted stairs leading down from the balcony

A pensive 16-year-old Stephen Boswell, 1963

'Anyway, it was around Halloween time of year and there was a fancy dress ball on at the Town Hall. While Lionel was working away the door at the back of the stalls suddenly opened and a man came in dressed in grey knee breeches. Lionel looked up and said, 'Can I help you? I think you want the Town Hall.' The figure turned, without saying anything, and walked out. Poor Lionel then realised that there was no way anyone could have got in because all the doors were locked. Anyway, that was enough for him and he packed up his music and left through the stage door which, of course, was still locked.'

Josephine also remembered the stage designer, Peter Brocket, who had joined the company with Ian Mullins in 1961. He would often work late at night on the paint frame, painting the set for the next show. He had seen the ghost of a little old lady in black and swore that the long, stone staircase that came down to ground level from the gods was haunted. 'Yes, that's right, he told me about that. Nobody would use that staircase, it was terribly cold.'

Robert Whelan had his own story to tell about that staircase. 'During stage parties we used to challenge each other to walk through that passage at the back of the Upper Circle. That was scary. I occasionally used to get an extra ten bob a week to light the emergency gas lights before the show and put them out after. It was that passage and the long stairs that were the scary bits.'

Iris Bailey, who worked as an usherette in the mid fifties, never saw a ghost but she wasn't keen on the passage either. 'It was very creepy in that corridor behind the Upper Circle. I was an impressionable fifteen-year-old schoolgirl and I would never go through there by myself.'

A thirteen-year-old Stephen Boswell felt a mysterious presence too. 'At the beginning of 1960, I helped my mother show the Everyman's first General Manager, Bill Bland Wood around an empty theatre one Sunday afternoon. I did not know of the theatre ghost then but we all felt the spooky atmosphere and I didn't want to linger long on my own but stayed close to the other two.'

Whelan recalls a particularly creepy night when he too was on the famous paint frame. 'During my Christmas holiday from Liverpool University in 1964 I helped the designer, Ray Hughes, paint the set for *Babes in the Wood*. After the show came down Ray, his assistant, Jean Robertson and I came into the theatre to work.

'The theatre was locked up and we were the only people there. The paint frame was across the back of the stage; a huge, wooden frame on which the scenery stood, and winched up and down with a winding gear on the fly floor and a large drum up in the grid. We went up to the paint frame by way of the prompt side fly floor and worked on the woodland back-cloth, painting leaves. I was mostly the labourer, heating the size and mixing the paint on the gas rings in the little corner.

'After a few hours we decided to have a break. It was sometime after one in the morning – maybe two o'clock. We made our way along the fly floor through the heavy fire door, past the offices and down the concrete stairs across the stage, lit only by the working light and into the kitchen. We settled down in the silent, cold, dusty old theatre with our tea.

'After a few minutes we heard the heavy steel fire door up on the prompt side fly floor slam close. We froze. There were footsteps along the fly floor. We looked at each other. The theatre was icy cold. We heard the paint spray machine start up. After a while – I've no idea how long – silence.

'Our tea was cold. 'Let's call it a day, eh?' said Ray. We agreed. We switched off the kitchen light and walked quickly across the dark stage. We had to unlock the stage door. We had been locked in and, we had thought, alone.'

Roger Hendry, who has been at the Everyman on and off since 1969, has done most of the jobs backstage and knows every nook and cranny of the place – and all the stories. One of the strangest is of the Victorian gentleman who Roger first encountered when they were preparing for the redevelopment of the theatre. It happened on 22nd March 1983, a date he remembers well. 'It was the day before my birthday, that's why I remember it. We were moving a safe down from what was the Café Bar. That was down the old circular staircase that was on the right of the foyer. There were seven or eight of us lowering it on ropes when suddenly this old man appears. We had no idea where he came from because the building was all locked up. What was unusual about him was his appearance. He was like an undertaker, very Victorian with long sideburns. He kept asking what play was on and we kept telling him the theatre was closed. He got a bit irate but finally said goodbye and went down the stairs.

'He had just got out of sight round the corner when one rope snapped. We all fell backwards and the safe went tumbling down. We went charging after it thinking it must have crushed the old man but when we got there he had disappeared. There was no way he could have got all the way down the stairs in those couple of seconds.'

But that wasn't the only incident with an old Victorian gentleman. Roger continued, 'There used to be an old painting that we used to decorate the sets sometimes. As time went on we realised that if

left: The hole in the back wall allegedly caused by the removal of the haunted painting.

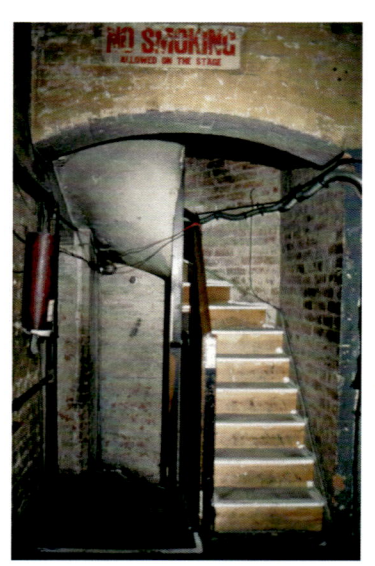

right: The stairs to the flies, stage left

this portrait was not on stage, something would go wrong with the performance. We finally nailed it to the back wall so it would always be there. On our last day before it was all demolished I was leaving the building with Carol Evans, who was the stage-manager, and she said 'I'm going to rescue the portrait'. and went back to get it. Two minutes after she took the painting down the wall collapsed leaving a great big hole. It was only then that I realised that this portrait was of the old man we had seen on the stairs'.

But there were other strange happenings backstage. 'There was supposed to be a ghost here,' Roger said, pointing to where the old kitchen used to be. 'He was a stage-hand who fell from the flies onto the old wooden stairs and was killed. He was known as John, the Human Counterweight. I knew the stairs creaked a bit but I never believed there was a ghost there.

'I used to work the tabs which used to be in the corner, alongside the old stairs to the flies. It was an old counterweight system that used to run up and down in a metal frame. There was a locking lever at the bottom and you would raise and lower the curtain by hand.

'Anyway, one evening I just couldn't get them to move. I was pulling and pulling the rope but they just wouldn't budge. I could hear this creaking on the staircase just behind me but I knew there was nobody there. Then Carol arrived and said, 'Say hello to John.' I said 'what?' She said, 'Say hello to John, quickly.' So I did. I said 'Hello John.' And all of a sudden the tabs just flew out by themselves without me touching them and the stairs started creaking again. 'That was John,' Carol said. Very strange and a bit scary.'

Malcolm Farquhar never saw anything during his time there but remembers those who did. 'There used to be the ghost of one of the old managers who used to live in the house next door which is now the bar and café. Apparently he was often seen in one of the boxes. Rae Hammond said that you'd always know if this old manager was watching during a dress rehearsal if the centre seat at the back of the upper circle flipped down.'

Farquhar also recalls an incident that happened in the same spot where Roger Hendry had trouble, next to the tab counter-weight. 'I had a stage manager once, a perfectly normal, sensible man who fled the theatre late one night during a fit-up. We found him standing outside the stage door, shaking like a leaf, refusing to come back in. He said he had been hammering something by the house tabs, when all of a sudden he was hit by this blast of freezing air and his hammer wouldn't move. I believed him because he was such a sensible soul.'

Wink Taylor remembers another story that Carol Evans used to tell. 'When I was first working at the Everyman in the early 1990s, Carol was the stage door keeper and she told me there was a ghost. She told me that a painter had once fallen to his death while painting the auditorium ceiling and that when she was alone, locked up in the theatre at night she would often hear whistling, which she believed was him.'

left: The winch in the stage-right flies used to raise and lower the paint frame

centre: The paint frame

right: The rope used to raise and lower the house tabs, which are just visible on the right

Whistling, along with quoting from *Macbeth*, is considered very unlucky in the theatre. The origins of this date back to when stage crews were often hired from ships in port. Theatrical rigging was originally devised by sailors. Both at sea and in the theatre they used a series of coded whistles to give instruction to those above, pulling the ropes. If you inadvertently whistled on stage your tune could be misinterpreted and you were quite likely to have something heavy dropped on your head.

Wink also remembers Carol Evans telling him that during the 1990s some real life ghost-busters had come into the theatre to investigate the ghost of an old actor that was sometimes seen in the dressing rooms. This was after the theatre was rebuilt; all the other stories, predictably, occurred before then.

The problem with ghost stories, like any others, is that the more they get told the more they get embellished and the more they change. One no longer knows which is the original story and which is not.

Robert Whelan claims he was told a similar tale, during a late night, back-stage ghost story session about the spectre of someone dressed as an Edwardian workman who had fallen to his death from the gods at the Theatre Royal, Bath. That, of course, along with all the others, was only a ghost story.

The following story is true and was reported in *The Gloucestershire Echo* on Monday 17th February 1919 and could well be the origin of the Bath story, Roger Hendry's 'human counterweight' and Carol Evans' phantom whistling. This is *The Echo* report in its entirety:

The final resting place of James John French in the churchyard in Charlton Kings, Cheltenham

photo: Caroline Borowski

A distressing fatality occurred at the Cheltenham Theatre while some workmen were engaged in cleaning operations. It was about 9.40a.m. and a man named James John French, a labourer in the employ of Mr. Charles H. Rainger, builder of 10 Bath Place, commenced the work of cleaning the wall in the Upper Circle. He was standing on some wooden steps about four feet from the front rail of the tier when he was seen to suddenly fall. Pitching on the front rail of the Dress Circle below, he then turned a somersault and dropped on his stomach on the back of the seats in the Pit-stalls.

A fellow workman named Hopson ran to his aid and, picking the unfortunate man up, laid him on the floor only, however, to find that he was dead. There were no external signs of injury to the head and on examination of the body at the mortuary whither it was conveyed by Police constables Attwood and Williams, a large bruise was found underneath the shoulder and also on the lower part of the spine which would seem to indicate that the poor fellow had broken his back in the fall. There were also slight scars on the side of each shin.

The cause of the accident can only be conjecture but the most probable explanation is that the steps were placed upon the seat and slipped when the man commenced his work, causing him to fall backwards. It is probable, too, that he met with his fatal injuries in the fall from the Upper Circle to the front rail of the Dress Circle and was dead when he reached the Pit. The total drop was 30 feet.

The final paragraph of the report stated that French was a married man with a wife and four grown-up children but his great-grand-daughter, Caroline Borowski, who came across the story while researching her family history, believes there were nine offspring. He lost one son in the Battle of Jutland and had two sons serving in the army, one in Egypt and the other in France.

The inquest was held at the police station in Crescent Place by coroner Mr. John Waghorne on Wednesday 19th February. French's daughter Mrs. Elizabeth White gave her father's age as 57 and stated that he enjoyed good health and was not subject to fits and that he lived at Church Place in Carlton Kings.

James French is buried in a simple, grass covered grave in the churchyard only a few yards from his home. His wife, who died six months later, is buried beside him. She had been committed to Gloucester Lunatic Asylum soon after his death being unable to cope with the loss she had suffered. Her death certificate states she died of 'exhaustion after fourteen days of mania'.

By a strange coincidence, Rainger was the name of the building contractor who had built John Boles Watson's Theatre Royal in Bath Place in 1805.

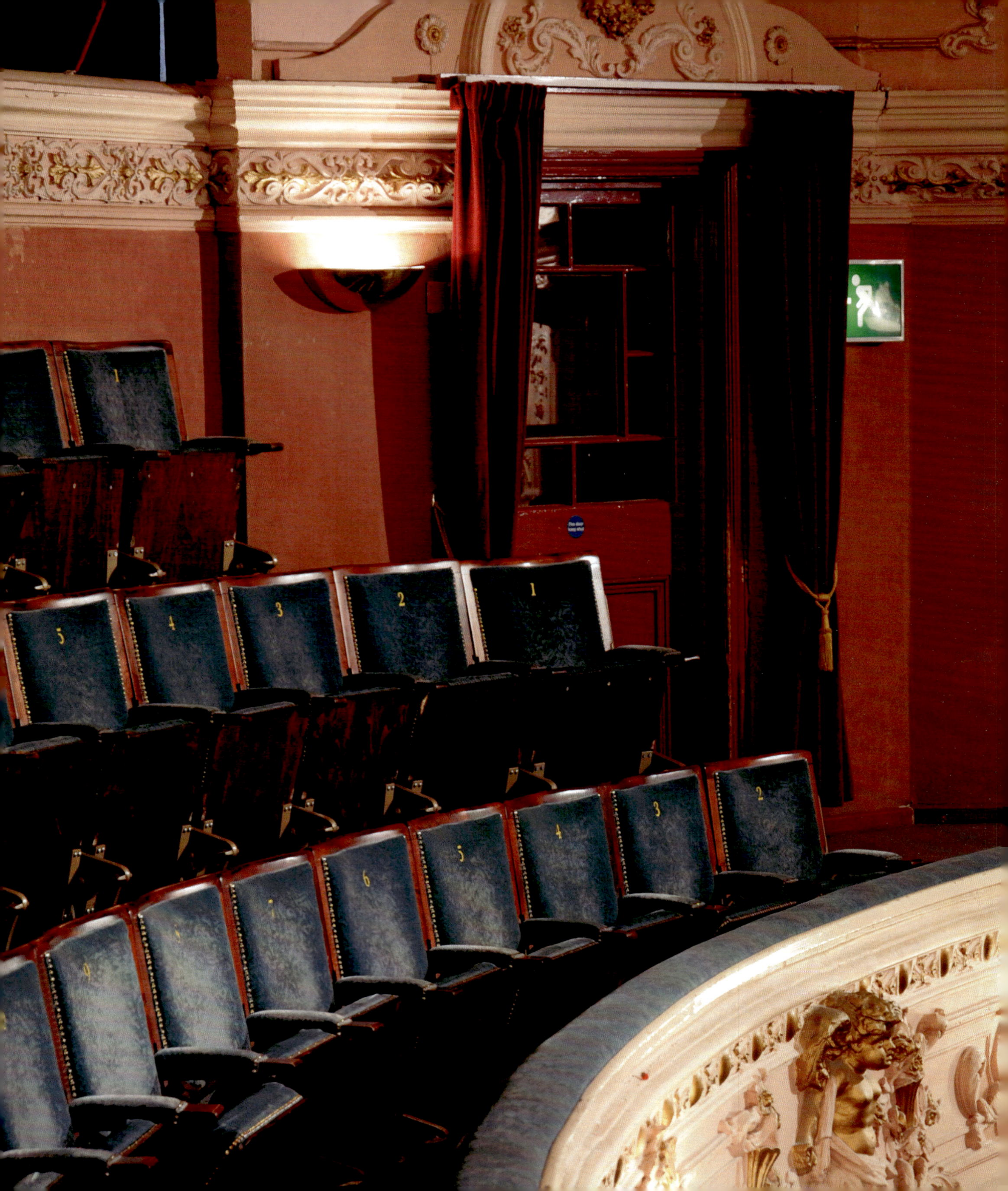

Chapter 13

Out, out brief candle
The Everyman is re-built 1983-1986

When the curtain fell for the last time onto the old stage on 26th February 1983 it was the end of an era. The boards that had been trodden by some of the greatest stars of the previous ninety-two years were torn up and the wings that had echoed with the voices of Richard Burton and John Gielgud fell silent.

The plan for the redevelopment of the theatre, then called merely 'a facelift,' was first announced in September 1980 as part of the £11m project by Cruden Developers for a 600 place, multi-storey car park and shopping mall to be known as The Regent Arcade. The company allocated £1.4m for the rebuilding of the backstage area of The Everyman which was to be incorporated into the main structure of the development. The scheme also involved the compulsory purchase and destruction of the Plough Hotel which had played such a part in the history of both the theatre and the town.

The theatre staff had until 22nd March 1983 to clear the building. The only things that were salvaged were the lights. Roger Hendry was one of the last people out. 'We handed the keys over to the Council, who owned the building, packed our bag and went. Some of us grabbed a few mementos but it was sad to see it go.' Within days, the grand old stage house was gone. The auditorium was completely sealed at the proscenium arch and was to remain so until the new stage house was complete.

The abandoned wings just before demolition

The door which led to the dressing rooms. The workshop was underneath

The skeleton staff that had been retained was keen that the audiences were not left completely high and dry and a group of them, under the leadership of Peter Denyer and John Hurt, decided to mount the Everyman pantomime of Christmas 1983 at the Town Hall. Roger Hendry has fond memories of Denyer. 'He was a good actor. After he first played the Everyman in the late seventies Malcolm rather took him under his wing. He did other things but, because he lived in Cheltenham, he was often around the theatre and he directed a few plays.'

'A group of us, Peter, John Hurt, Donald Crosby, Roger Barrett and I decided to keep the Everyman name alive and mount the pantomime at the Town Hall. The first one we did was *Aladdin*. It was a nightmare but great fun. We made the sets out of cardboard round at Sherborne Place and Donald painted them. We even built a proscenium arch.

We did it properly and professionally. I got a couple of my old stage-hand mates to come and help rig the lights and whatever – we used the lights we'd put in storage round at Dobells. Peter Denyer cast the show with himself as dame. It was brilliant, absolutely brilliant. Sold out every night. We had all the effects – dry ice, pyros blowing things up. It was just like the real thing'.

The new Artistic Director, John Doyle, started work in July 1985, his job initially was to oversee the completion of the new theatre and the creation of the new company.

He was responsible for all the fitting-out of the new back-stage area, everything from buying the lamps and lighting console to the choice of ironing board. 'When I arrived none of the dressing rooms, offices etc. were built, nor was the front of house. I was responsible for collaborating with the architect on all of these matters. Wearing a yellow hard-hat is a good experience for a young director.'

Doyle often got frustrated at the lack of progress. 'At times it almost seemed impossible to get the damn place finished. There were always disputes between architects and contractors in the normal fashion of any building project.' And, if the normal, predictable construction problems weren't enough… 'The roof even got burned down at one point – a maddening accident that nearly stopped the whole thing all together. These are stories that will go with me to my grave. Don't forget, during this time we were also trying to plan an opening season for two spaces, staffing the place, casting, doing publicity and everything else that goes with forming a company'.

One thing that was quite an improvement on the old backstage area was the allocation of a proper, purpose built Green Room; an area where actors could relax between scenes, have a chat, circulate a bit

The 1983 Everyman pantomime Aladdin was presented at the Town Hall

of gossip and make themselves a cup of tea. The new Green Room was clean, spacious and light. It had a television, a proper kitchen, microwave and even a terrace. The bad news was that it was about as far away from the stage as you could get without actually leaving the building.

The old dark and airless Green Room that David Gilmore had so loved and later, the Duchess Charles, were certainly not ideal spaces but at least they were within touching distance of the stage.

Seven meters below the new fly floor, the new stage was also state of the art. For one thing, it is possible to comfortably walk underneath it without bending double. The old Victorian trap doors and mechanisms had gone long before the theatre closed, but in their place the new stage consisted of an intricate system of rostrums which could be raised or lowered on hydraulic lifts to accommodate the demands of any visiting production.

Technical Stage Manager Kieran Barker explained the new system. 'There are twelve panels measuring eight by four feet making up the stage. Any of those can be moved or taken out so you can have a trap door wherever you want it. The under-stage area also acts as the band room when there's an orchestra'.

The front of house had acquired 10 Regent Street and this former home of the manager, Wilfred Simpson, was turned into the café, bar and restaurant. In order to access this new annex, the old staircase

130   Chapter 13   Out, out brief candle

The old stage house just before demolition in 1983. The Regent Arcade is rising from the ground on the right.

The back wall of the stage prior to demolition. The stage and an old back cloth is visible through the hole.

which ran up the common wall had to go. It was replaced with an unattractive concrete staircase which rose from the ground floor to the balcony taking up half the space of an already cramped foyer.

The theatre did not become habitable until January 1986, only a couple of weeks before the Studio Theatre opened at the end of February. 'Even then it wasn't completely ready,' remembers John Doyle. 'They were still using pneumatic drills outside the Studio as we were doing the dress rehearsal for the first play, *Peer Gynt*'.

But the Studio itself was not ideal and had been a rather an unhappy compromise. Malcolm Farquhar recollects how it came about. 'When we were planning the changes, well before the closure, they tried to foist this rehearsal room on us. I said we don't need a rehearsal room, we can use the stage. I wanted a decent studio theatre which could have been housed at the side, in the new extension that later became the café and bar. But no, the Arts Council would not sanction it and we finished up with a rehearsal room which nobody wanted, stuck up in the car park. At least my successor managed to change their minds.'

Chapter 13 Out, out brief candle

Gloucestershire Everyman Theatre

Welcome Back

BOX OFFICE
Cheltenham (0242) 572573

Doyle said at the time of the reopening, 'The opening of the main theatre will mean that at last we have our two venues working side by side at the Everyman. The Richardson Studio has already played to a capacity three and a half week run with *Peer Gynt* and we hope that its audience will continue to come back for more. *My Fair Lady* has done phenomenal advance booking and seems to have set things off to a good start. However, the life of a theatre is more about its continuation than its opening. The glamour of opening nights and Gala occasions must not overshadow the fact that we are a working, producing repertory company with a long programme of work ahead of us.

'Gloucestershire now has a beautiful and comfortable theatre with excellent catering and bar facilities, good provision for disabled patrons and improved heating and ventilation systems all of which go towards a more pleasant evening's entertainment. There has been a lot said for and against the whole project – I am pleased to say that those who were 'for', won the day'.

Roger Hendry has memories of the difficulties involved prior re-opening. 'We built the set for *My Fair Lady* in the theatre's Hewlett Road premises which we used as a workshop. At that time there was nowhere in the unfinished theatre that we could use. Parts of the new building would become available a bit at a time, as they were finished.'

Mick Gemson, the new stage electrician, remembers working to get the Studio ready. 'We were fitting out the Studio and brought in all the scaffolding to build the lighting grid in a van through the Regent Arcade car park. When we'd finished we turned the van round and headed out. But we couldn't get out; the van wouldn't go under the top of the door. All the scaffolding had been so heavy it had made the van much lower. The only way we could get out was to fill the van with stage weights and let down all the tyres'.

In spite of all the problems, all the delays and near catastrophes, the Everyman was more or less ready to open its doors at the start of a brand new era for the theatre.

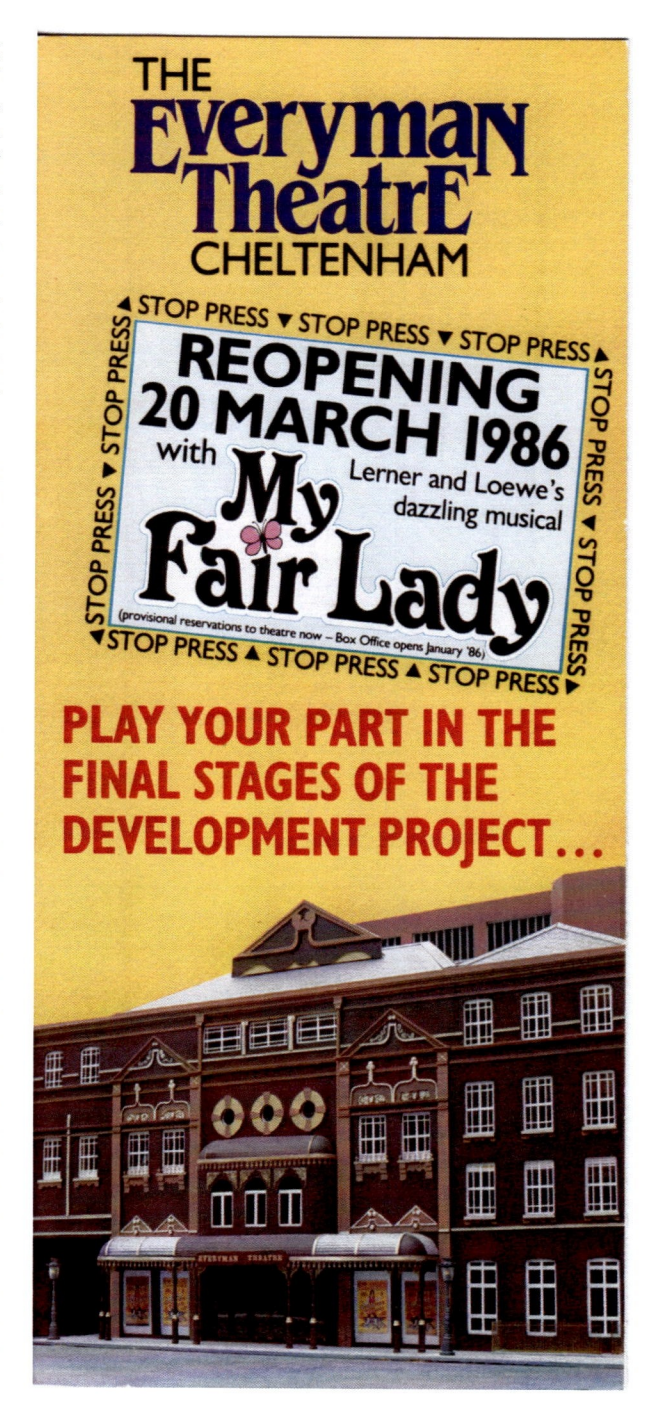

EVERYMAN CHELTENHAM 1891 CENTENARY 1991

TALES FROM KITES HILL
A GLOUCESTERSHIRE FANTASY

Chapter 14

The Winds of Change
The final years of the rep 1986-1995

When the theatre proper reopened in March 1986 it was a completely different place. Although the auditorium had remained more or less the same, the front of house had been spoiled. The new, ugly concrete staircase, more suitable for a football stadium, left the foyer cramped and unattractive.

The new façade however, was a vast improvement on the old-fashioned straight lines, glass and gaudy colours of the sixties. A facsimile of the original brickwork had been reinstated on the first floor and an attractive, Victorian-style wrought iron canopy installed along the width of the building.

Of the old backstage area nothing remained. It was now all new, clean and efficient. There were spacious offices, dressing-rooms with showers, a flying system that did not need three men to operate it, a workshop that did not involve leaving the building to access and a stage door keeper to keep an eye on everything. Gone were the cramped spaces, dusty corners, inadequate facilities and creaky, hundred-year-old equipment.

But gone too was the patina, the history that was embedded in the walls and every nook and cranny behind the proscenium arch. But, most importantly, what had been lost was the continuity. After three years closure, the line that stretched all the way back to 1891 and Lillie Langtry had been broken. Everything was effectively starting from year zero.

Roger Hendry, who had been around for seventeen years, was reinstated as Technical Production Manager and Carol Evans, the former stage manager, became stage-door keeper. Manager John Hurt and scenic designer Donald Crosby also came back, but neither were to last very long. But everything and everyone else was new and it would never be the same. Some of the actors and technicians were brought down from John Doyle's previous theatre, the Swan in Worcester.

For Doyle it must have been almost like presiding over the opening of a completely new theatre rather than one that had a history going back nearly ninety years. 'In some senses that's true. However, every choice that was made was made in relation to the past history of the place.'

Donald Crosby saw it differently. 'I wasn't happy about how the theatre was run. It just made me mad. I'm still very emotional about it; it had been such a wonderful part of my life. Since I walked out of the Everyman for the last time in 1995 I have not been in a theatre again, not one theatre. I can't do it. That's how upset I was.'

Doyle was aware of the problems. 'It was no easy task taking the job on, as there was much local negative reaction to the change of regime. The reality is, that the funding bodies would have been unlikely to support the continuation of the repertory had there been no change in the directorate.

Craig Rogers and Lucy Gill in *Half a Sixpence* by Everyman Youth Theatre, October 1994
Photo: Alan Wood

'I felt very sorry for Malcolm Farquhar and I personally took much of the local flack. There was much tension between the past and the present, much of which was exaggerated by the press and quite unfounded'. Roger Hendry confirms that not everybody was happy. 'There was a very bad undertone about what was happening with the changeover. Everybody was expecting Malcolm to come back and it was a bit of shock to find out that he wasn't'.

The Cheltenham Council weren't happy either. There had been a large overspend on the project which threatened to become a party political issue according to *The Stage*. The Audit Commission and the Royal Institute of Chartered Surveyors were brought in at the end of the year to check the figures and lay the blame for what was reckoned to be a £700,000 overspend.[1] One of the factors was certainly the roof fire that occurred during building and the delays it caused.

The fire had set the whole rebuilding project back about three months and Doyle was keen to get the theatre open. It was decided to present the first play in the Studio.

Everyman Theatre Company

THE Country Wife

Thursday 14 – Saturday 30 April

A bawdy costume comedy by William Wycherley

WITH THE ASSISTANCE OF SOUTH WEST ARTS

BOX OFFICE (0242) 572573
EVERYMAN
Everyman Theatre
Regent Street Cheltenham GL50 1HQ

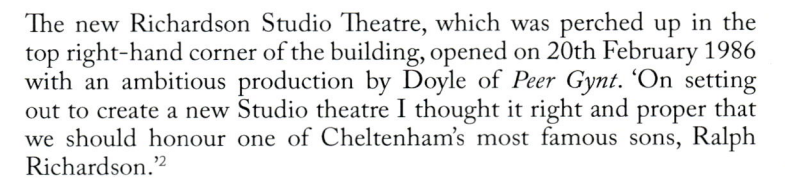

The new Richardson Studio Theatre, which was perched up in the top right-hand corner of the building, opened on 20th February 1986 with an ambitious production by Doyle of *Peer Gynt*. 'On setting out to create a new Studio theatre I thought it right and proper that we should honour one of Cheltenham's most famous sons, Ralph Richardson.'[2]

Doyle's choice of *Peer Gynt* to open the new Studio was no accident. The production at the New Theatre in London's St. Martin's Lane in 1944, with Sir Ralph playing the title role alongside Laurence Olivier and Sybil Thorndike, was a triumph. Richardson said of the role 'Peer Gynt is one of my favourite parts. I have a great liking for the character'.

Roger Hendry remembers it too. 'It was a promenade production, that is, the audience moved around with the action. We had to construct a mountain which people had to climb up and down. It had to be built from scratch, in situ. There was no workshop and when the timber was delivered, the truck just dumped it on the pavement in Regent Street. We had to carry it all up the main staircase piece by piece.

'There were bits of scenery by the main door which the actors had to squeeze past. Little of the front of house was ready so the box office consisted of a cash register on a table and we had a makeshift bar.'

The Stage gave *Peer Gynt* a good review but confirmed the state of the theatre. 'With the paint hardly dry, the Everyman Theatre, Cheltenham has at last got a foot in the stirrup. With the new Richardson Studio Theatre fully equipped it is currently back in business with Henrik Ibsen's *Peer Gynt*. The Studio ... though small and at present rather uncomfortable – if not downright primitive – burns with an anticipation of the grand reopening of the main building ...'[3]

The main house finally opened on 20th March 1986 with a gala performance of *My Fair Lady*. The spectacular production starred Jacqueline Dankworth, daughter of John Dankworth and Cleo Laine. The performance was attended by Princess Anne and her husband, Captain Mark Phillips.

Doyle's associate, Phyllida Lloyd, directed several plays in the first couple of years of the new company including Dario Fo's *Accidental Death of an Anarchist*, Alan Ayckbourne's *Just Between Ourselves* and *What the Butler Saw* by Joe Orton. After Cheltenham, she went on to a long and distinguished career including directing both the West End production and film of *Mama Mia*.

In recognition of her contribution to British theatre, Phyllida Lloyd was awarded a CBE in the 2010 New Year Honours.

Wenda Holland as the Fairy and Paul Milton as Simple Simon in *Sleeping Beauty*, 1987

Sheila Mander, who was later to become an Associate Director herself, remembers Ms. Lloyd well. 'As with John Doyle, Cheltenham was very much a stepping stone for her. She did some wonderful work here, often with me in the education department. She's one of those women who have huge talent but she's not a bit snobbish about where she puts it and she was always willing to come in on workshop and schools days and was excellent. I learned a lot from Phyllida.'

To mark the first anniversary of his tenure, John Doyle mounted an ambitious production of *West Side Story*. Its cast included a young Paul Milton who had worked with Doyle in Worcester and was to become a regular member of the company. Paul would return to the Everyman in 2009 as Director of ReachOut where part of his responsibilities would include running the Studio Theatre. In 2011 he was appointed Artistic Director of the Everyman. He rated Doyle very highly. 'All his shows were lavish. He did these big mega-shows and managed to find or create audiences that hadn't existed before. He was packing the theatre out. The Everyman got this reputation for doing these big provincial musicals.

'We built up an incredible reputation and people would travel a long way to see the shows and it wasn't just musicals. John did some amazing things. I saw a production in the Studio of *Hedda Gabler*. The audience were actually in the set, sitting on her settee with her. It was phenomenal what he was doing, real groundbreaking stuff'.

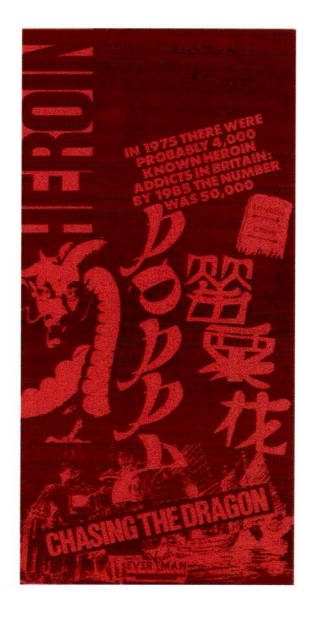

EVERYMAN YOUTH THEATRE:

left: *Chasing the Dragon*, 1987

right; Costume designs for *Fiddler on the Roof*, 1996

In 1984, Sheila Mander, who had trained at the Guildhall Drama School in the early fifties and qualified as a teacher at the same time, created the Everyman Youth Theatre. 'I was living in Cheltenham and after my family had grown up, I contacted John Doyle suggesting I could do some workshops. At the end of the interview he asked me if I'd be prepared to work part-time and to start a youth theatre and an education department, which I did. I gradually became full time. The first show I did with the Youth Theatre was *Our Day Out* which was in the Studio and the first show we did in the main house in 1997 was the first part of the R.S.C.'s *Nicholas Nickleby*'.

The ReachOut scheme was created that year and involved visiting schools and youth groups and creating workshops with professional actors. Another significant event for the new Youth Theatre was the establishment by the National Theatre of a scheme to encourage young people in the theatre. Sheila Mander was involved in *Connections* right from the start. 'I suggested that they should commission twelve plays and then offer them to youth groups all over the country for them to produce in their own school or whatever and then the local regional theatre would give them an opportunity to air them in their building. The National would choose the twelve best from around the country which would go forward to take part in the event in London. The best thing that happened with the Youth Theatre, apart from *Connections*, was that we visited lots of places. We took our version of the Anne Frank story to Amsterdam and played it in her house. We also had an exchange arrangement with a group in Italy'.

left: Zigger Zagger, 1993

right: Fiddler on the Roof, 1996

In 1986, the Town Hall was undergoing fairly major restoration work itself and again the Everyman played host to the Literature Festival. But it was not a great success, again because of the cramped conditions. The lack of open spaces and their restrictive size necessitated the popular Children's Book Festival being held at The Axiom in nearby Winchcombe Street.

There was a popular innovation at the theatre in 1987 when it was decided to provide a canteen service in the new Green Room. Alison Greening was appointed to run it. 'I started here on 1st February 1987. I answered an advert for a cook. They wanted someone to run the Green Room and cook the actors' lunches. I did that for seven years during which time Carol Evans ran the stage door.'

One of the high spots of John Doyle's reign was a spectacular production of Shakespeare's *Twelfth Night* in February/March 1989. People still talk about the play and the two words that always crop up are 'swimming pool'.

The play was set in a sort of holiday resort in the Adriatic and a real live pool was the main feature of the set which had been designed by Chris Croswell. Carol Turnham had been a regular visitor to the Everyman since she was a teenager in the mid-sixties. It was that production of *Twelfth Night* that she still remembers. 'At the time I was employed by a firm of architects and my memory of the swimming pool is of complete wonder as to the practicality of how they did it. It was great watching them having fun up there on the stage, jumping in and making great splashes over the others and over the stage, yet still managing to keep word-perfect. Absolutely fantastic'.

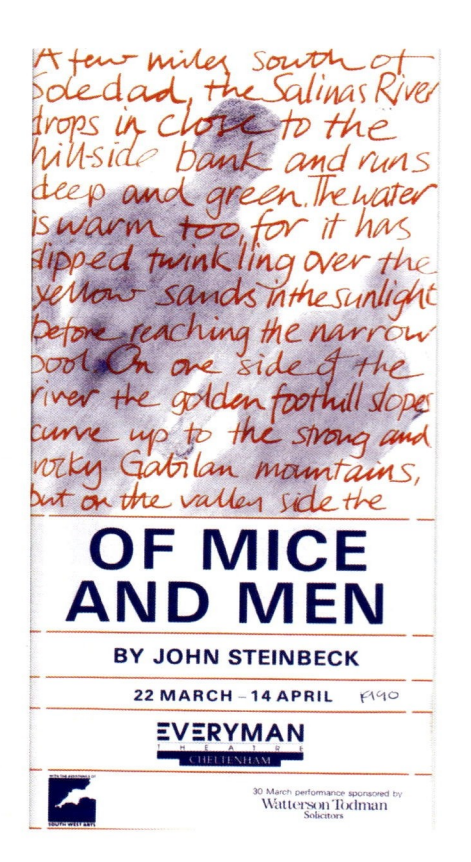

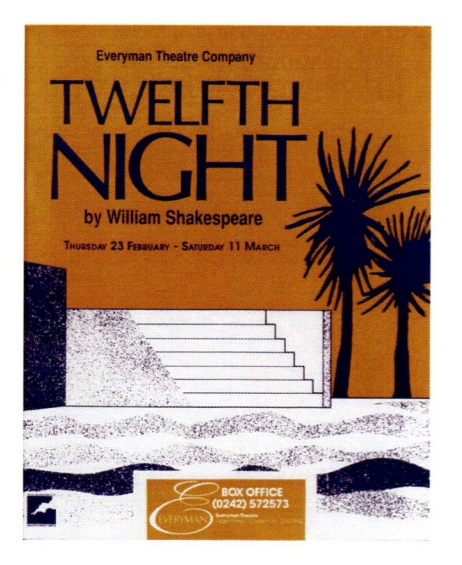

Roger Hendry remembers the show. 'Most of the action took place in the pool with the actors having to tread water. I don't know how they did it. If you were sitting in the dress circle or the upper circle it was great but if you were in the stalls you couldn't see much. We built that pool from scratch. It was nine feet deep, all the way from the stage level down to the floor beneath. When we'd finished we had to get the fire brigade to come and pump it out. A few weeks later we had to fill the orchestra pit with water to represent a river in *Of Mice and Men*. We did some wonderful things here.'

By the time John Doyle left the Everyman at the end of the 1988/9 season the theatre had debts, according to Doyle, of about £50,000. A lot of money was spent on sets and Roger Hendry remembers that they were hardly ever re-used. 'When a show finished the sets were often taken up to Hewlett Road and dumped, rarely to be used again. Most the scenery during that time was new-build. But I have to admit some of the sets were wonderful.'

Paul Milton does not consider that money was ever wasted. 'I honestly don't believe it was. The thing is, you can't do *West Side Story* with less than twenty actors and actors are expensive. *The King and I* has to be lavish. John was very successful in terms of audience figures. He would do these big shows, three or four a year, and as soon as they were announced, they would sell out.'

It was certainly a far cry from the old days of rep in the sixties when sets would be recycled and the same old windows, doors and stairs would been re-arranged and given a new coat of paint for each play. Furniture, much of it borrowed, would make regular appearances with different cushions or coverings. Times had changed and had got a lot more expensive.

Doyle was succeeded by Martin Houghton. Houghton had trained at the Drama Centre in London and had founded the Northumberland Theatre Company in 1977 and was their artistic director until 1985. He then worked freelance and, immediately prior to taking up the job at the Everyman, had been Associate Director at the Theatre Royal, York.[4]

'It was clear at the interview that they wanted changes made. I came in on a very open and honest ticket, I made it quite clear I was committed to community theatre and I would try and set up a quick touring circuit. I also told them I would invest money in education and that I was quite keen to develop what was already a thriving youth theatre. The main object was to try and shift the profile of the audience and try and get a younger profile into the building. And, to that end, the first appointment I made was to make Sheila Mander an Associate Director to try and emphasise the priorities'.

Houghton then set up a grid which was a circuit of non-theatre venues throughout Gloucestershire as part of the theatre's commitment to the community and education development programme. With Martin Houghton's appointment, it seems the Board was keen to continue the programme of adventurous and innovative productions. But Houghton, it seems, was surprised to get the job. 'To be honest, I didn't think I had a cat in hell's chance of getting it.'

One of the most significant appointments that Houghton made, and one that was to impact on the theatre until the demise of the rep, was a new designer. 'The other important thing I did then was to bring Nettie Edwards on board as Head of Design. Her work is visually quite extraordinary.

I also appointed Michael E. Hall to create the lighting. The three of us really aimed to create the artistic hub. The work was quite physical, visceral and at times quite sexy.'

All well and good, but one show you don't expect to be sexy is probably *The Sound of Music*. The opening of the show no doubt raised a few eyebrows; Julie Andrews it certainly wasn't. Houghton described what happened. 'We opened *The Sound of Music* with Maria coming out of a pool and dressing while she sang *The Hills are Alive*. It was very beautiful I have to say and it was very delicately lit, you wouldn't have known she was naked, she was silhouetted. But anyway she was in a body stocking at the time.' However, he does concede, 'There was outrageous work that went on as well'.

Paul Milton remembers Houghton. 'He went in a slightly different direction; he went down a route that was even more avant-garde than John Doyle. He was very off the wall'.

'He never did conventional scenery either,' recalls Hendry. 'We did a production of *The Importance of Being Ernest* and one of the sets was a giant cut-away teapot and another, a handbag.' Paul Milton remembers that too, 'It was like a Salvador Dali painting, bizarre'. Sheila Mander says, 'Some of the best things about Martin's shows were the designs by Nettie Edwards which were fabulous. Many of them were quite extraordinary'.

Martin Houghton and Nettie Edwards would work hand in hand over the next five years, their functions at times even seeming to merge, with Nettie being involved in all aspects of the production.

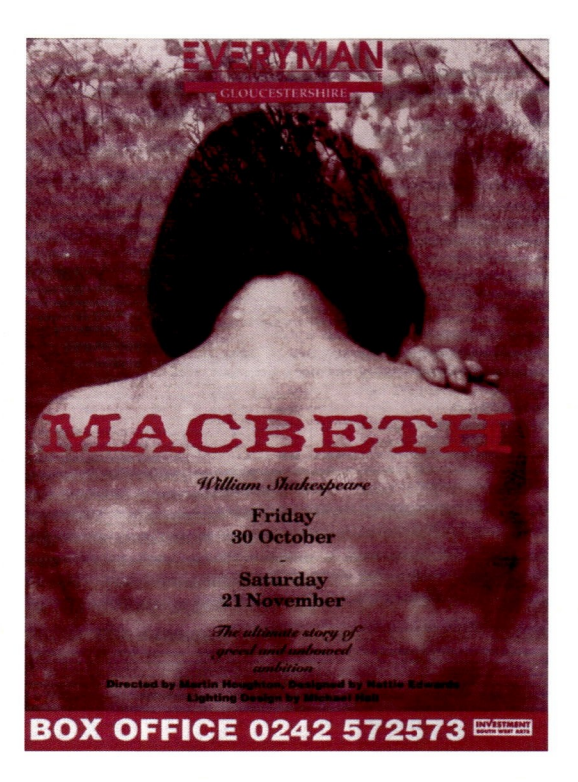

Michael Hall, along with Houghton and Edwards, completed the creative triumvirate, a team which was to be one of the most imaginative, visually original and also the most controversial in the theatre's history.

Fine Time Fontayne joined the company as an actor and associate director and became a calming influence when the waters became choppy. Sheila Mander has fond memories, 'Fine Time was a wonderful person to have in the building. He would wear bow-ties and peculiar things; he'd always be a bit quirky. He was a lovely company member and that was needed at the time. When things got a bit spikey and there was a sort of erratic leadership, Fine Time provided a wonderful element of sanity. He brought with him a sense of fun and it was good to have him around'.

Actor Tony Caunter has good memories of Cheltenham and of working with Houghton. 'Of the many directors with whom I have worked over the last thirty eight years as a professional actor, including experience on the West End and New York stage, I can honestly say that I have found working under Martin's aegis to be one of the most stimulating and rewarding experiences I have had as a performer. He

Nettie Edwards' designs for *Macbeth*, 1992

constantly encourages his actors to find other ways of approaching a role, while at the same time, being thoroughly supportive and constructive. He never imposes his will, preferring that the actor should find his/her own way to the truth of a performance. An actor is never allowed to take the easy way out and yet Martin rarely seems to criticize.

'He has a wide and vivid imagination, often approaching a particular situation or problem from an oblique angle and is happiest when the actor is taking risks. The performer is never allowed to 'rest on his laurels'; Martin continues to seek the utmost from you until the reins are taken from his hands'.

1991 was an eventful year for the Everyman. Not only did it mark the theatre's centenary but it had two productions and an actor nominated for national awards. *Auction* by Jean Binnie, which premiered at the Everyman in February that year, was nominated in the Best Regional Theatre Writing category of The Writers' Guild Awards.

But it was not all good news. In April the theatre, again, was teetering on the brink of disaster. Nearly half of the Board, including chairman

Christopher Powell, abruptly resigned after predictions of mounting deficit. The board had been warned by accountants that they could be personally held liable for the £30,000 debt under the terms of the 1986 Insolvency Act. South West Arts stepped in to save the day but did not allocate extra money for 1991/2. Instead, they guaranteed that the £240,000 package already on offer would be awarded in one lump sum, rather than in monthly instalments, if the theatre was forced to close.[5]

Writing in a 1992 programme, Houghton said, 'Hundreds of people in villages and towns all around Gloucestershire who have enjoyed visits over the past three years from the Everyman Theatre's Community Touring Programme will be relieved to know that, this autumn at least, the show will go on – with the fourth Everyman Community Tour, *Laurel and Hardy* by Tom McGrath'.

1992 was a very good creative year for the theatre and probably Houghton's most successful, being twice nominated for the year's prestigious TMA Regional Theatre Awards. He was nominated Best Director for his production of *Who's Afraid of Virginia Woolf* and his production of Ostrovsky's *A Family Affair* was nominated Best Production.

At the beginning of 1993, major changes were made to the way the theatre was run. Bubble Lodge, who since 1990 had been the administrator, was made Chief Executive with total responsibility for running the theatre, a post above that of Artistic Director who would normally have over all charge. The chairman of the Board at the time, Hugh Raymond, stated that Martin Houghton had been given a further three year contract '… so the Artistic Direction of the Everyman remains in excellent hands'.[6]

At around the same time, four members of the Youth Theatre – Neal Wright, Kate Mander, Paula Stephens and Ross Andrews were invited to the Royal National Theatre to attend a Masterclass held by Sir Anthony Hopkins on 18th March.

This prestigious invitation came about when Sir Anthony learnt of the plight of many young hopefuls who, having been offered a place at an accredited drama school, were unable to take up the opportunity because of the lack of grant aid for drama students.

At the end of April 1993 The Everyman Theatre staged a brand new play, an adaptation of Charlotte Bronte's *Jane Eyre* written by Nick Jones and directed by Martin Houghton. Nick Jones was born in Cheltenham in 1948 and educated at Cheltenham Grammar School from where he gained a scholarship to St. John's College, Cambridge.

Nick said of his adaptation, 'My version tries to include as much as possible of the richness and sweep of Bronte's tale. I also wanted to write a version of *Jane Eyre* which would complement the particular talents of the Everyman's artistic team'.

His first ever play, *Piece en Morceaux – But More So,* was performed at the Everyman in 1966 by the Cheltenham Youth Theatre. As an adult writer, his *Tales from Kite's Hill*, directed by Fine Time Fontayne, had a very successful community tour by the Everyman company after premiering in The Richardson Studio in April 1991.

By December 1994, the theatre's financial difficulties were reaching crisis point. Philip Bernays, an experienced theatre administrator, was brought in as a consultant to try and sort things out. 'When I arrived, initially for a three month consultancy, both Martin Houghton and the Chief Executive were away for some reason. I'm not quite sure of the circumstances.

'I'd just left the Young Vic in London and was working freelance. The Board at the Everyman called me in, I think, to hold the reins for few months. When I arrived I went through the figures and it was clear to me that the theatre was losing money and had a deficit. Basically I came to the conclusion that the rep model was just unsustainable. The truth was there just wasn't enough funding and given the size of the auditorium, there is only so much you can earn. Any gap is made up with funding. From what I could gather, the Everyman had, historically, never been a well funded theatre; it had always been a bit of a hand to mouth existence.

'Although Ian Mullins and Malcolm Farquhar had kept the place afloat, I think the expectations of what a rep did and what a rep does had shifted somewhat over the course of the nineties and beyond from popular to more esoteric theatre, I suppose. The rep system as we knew it, which had gone back decades, was changing and the Everyman did not have the funding to keep pace with that change.

'One of the problems was audience expectations of what they could see. The expectations had been raised by film and television and with television stars, especially those from the soaps, touring with popular plays.'

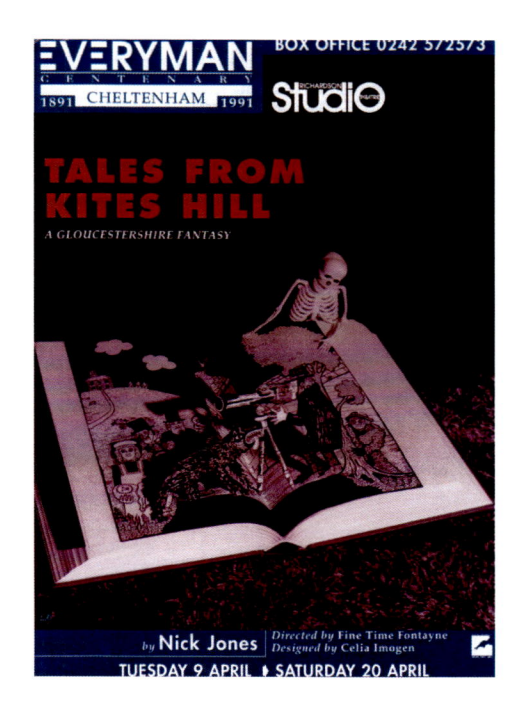

It was always going to be difficult for theatres, especially rep theatres to compete with television, as it had with films in the thirties. Audiences like to see familiar faces and to a great extent reps provided them; it was not that different from supporting your local football team. However, with television and the increasingly popular soap-operas, not only did the viewers have faces they could become familiar with, but relatively expensive and always varying settings.

Reps constantly struggled with very limiting budgets and in the end could not compete with the flickering screen in people's living rooms and with a world that had moved on. And there was frequently the problem with reconciling artistic endeavour and integrity with the demands and restriction imposed by Boards of Directors.

There are often problems between creative people trying to be creative and boards, often businessmen, trying to run a business. They both look down the same tube, but from different ends and they each have their own agenda. This had been a problem at the theatre since the rep had been established in 1960 and continued right through until its very last day. And if two different viewpoints were not enough, the Arts Council who held the purse strings, had another one.

From an audience's point of view, the Everyman had been going through one of its most exciting and creative periods, but along with that came problems. From the very beginning Houghton had trouble with the board. 'In the long run we didn't bring in the numbers needed quickly enough to match the cost of the operation. I think there is a danger in calling the work we did experimental. This of course created major problems with the board.

'In spite of my interview and my track record it seemed as though they had no idea of what I was going to deliver. They had no cultural awareness whatsoever. I was already getting terribly exhausted by the nature of these [board] meetings. It seemed to me that very few of the Board ever came to see the plays and that in itself was a statement of how they felt.'

By the end of 1994 it all got too much for Houghton and he had a breakdown. 'I just collapsed in the office one day. I was absolutely exhausted. I went home to recover; I was away for about three weeks I think. The story is horrid, during that time they decided to dump us. The chairman of the Board came to see me and told me they had decided to close the rep.

'This was before Philip Bernays arrived and I think, without a doubt, they had made up their mind long before Philip came and did all the calculations. They offered me a very paltry sum to end my contract and I wasn't in a very good state to argue it and the Union took my case up. But it wasn't just me, it was happening all over the place. There were quite a few of the reps that were in deep trouble.' In spite of the creative and visually spectacular work he produced at the Everyman,

Houghton does not remember his time at Cheltenham with fondness. 'It was a nightmare from day one. At the end of the day I believed that I had been foisted on the Everyman by the Arts Council which is why I was given such a hard time.

'Nevertheless, I think the work I did on stage was of a superb standard. I think the acting was superb and the standard of presentation was extraordinary. Nettie's work and the work of all the team was outstanding. I was extremely proud of all the work we did, every one of the shows that we did had exceptional production values and I thought it deserved better treatment in the end. I thought we were poorly treated, Nettie in particular.'

The axe finally fell at the beginning of 1995 and Martin Houghton was out. *The Stage* was reporting that a total of ten jobs were to go with a saving over three years of £400,000.

At the beginning of March 1995, Houghton, along with director Michael Hunt who had stepped in while Houghton was ill, slammed the Board of the Everyman claiming the theatre was being run 'like a second-hand car yard'. They both demanded the Board's resignation claiming it was 'a mess of bureaucracy'. There was bickering over the size of the deficit, Hunt claiming one figure, Bernays another. And Bernays was clearly not supporting the demand for the Board to resign. He said, 'What individual members of the Board decide to do is up to them but none have acted improperly'.[7] It was all getting a bit acrimonious and there was just the smallest hint of *déjà vu* about it all.

With nobody at the artistic helm, to some, the theatre seemed to be drifting. Soon after the Hunt/Houghton demand, Equity members employed on short-term contracts at the theatre demanded that a new artistic director be appointed as soon as possible. In an open letter, cast members of the three shows playing at the time wanted as much in-house work as possible produced until January 1997. They also wanted a commitment that, after that period, a full rep company be restored and maintained.

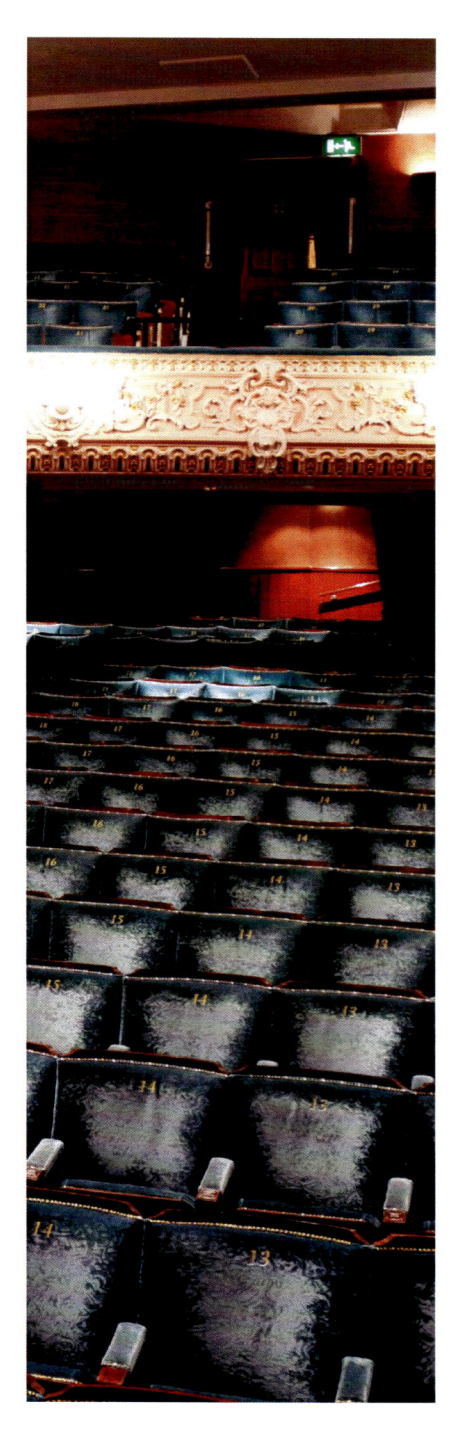

Those involved stated that, because they were not on long term contracts, they were not consulted regarding matters that concerned their livelihoods. Philip Bernays told them, 'We have every sympathy with Equity members and indeed all staff at the theatre and can assure them our aim is to keep live theatre in Cheltenham. We will be largely receiving tours for the next eighteen months and have the fullest commitment to returning to rep after that time'.[8] Despite the assurance he gave in 1995, when interviewed in 2010 Bernays made it clear that there never had been any real chance of a return to rep. 'A sizeable deficit had accumulated over the previous few years so the object of the exercise, the reason I had been called in, was to get the theatre back on an even keel and reduce the debt. The conclusion of my report was that the rep should end and for the Everyman to become a receiving house. By that time public support for the rep was dwindling and it more or less just fizzled out.'

The truth was that, in fact, the rep at the Everyman had had a very good innings. By the mid nineties most of the other weekly or fortnightly reps around the country had disappeared. Geoffrey Rowe, who was to succeed Philip Bernays as Chief Executive, had witnessed the changes in regional theatre over the past few years. 'The Arts Council had a policy of requiring the theatres they funded to go to three-weekly rep and moving its funding to large areas of conurbation and favouring those theatres, like Bristol for example.

They were also keen on setting up new theatres where none existed, like the Manchester Royal Exchange or the West Yorkshire Playhouse. They also supported theatres that had established some unique identity like Stoke and Scarborough and, frankly, a level of artistic success.

'Cheltenham satisfied none of these criteria. Three-weekly rep meant that you needed far more people to see each production at a time when there were fewer willing to sign up for a season ticket to see 10 or 12 shows a year, especially at a time when cinema and television were commanding people's time.

Philip Bernays in 2005
photo: Michael Hasted

'Another aspect was that there were major industrial changes in the theatre. It may be very romantic to think of 16-year-olds from the Grammar School in charge of the flying system but clearly that was no longer possible and the theatre became more professional and everyone had to be paid properly. Equity had managed to establish a maximum 48 hour week along with a whole range of other improvements including one that stipulated that stage-managers should not act [in plays]. This forced out the theatres that were reliant on people working incredibly long hours and some people working for nothing.'

When the rep finished at Cheltenham, Philip Bernays announced there were 'a few, but thankfully not many' redundancies. He explained, 'It was near the end of a season and I think most of the stage management were on seasonal contracts, so there weren't too many problems'.

One very long serving member of the Everyman staff who had already left at about this time was stage-door keeper Carol Evans who had been at the theatre since the late seventies. Her place was taken by Alison Greening. 'When Carol left I took over the stage door and the Green Room canteen stopped. By that time the theatre was a receiving house so there weren't enough people in the building during the day to justify it.'

In early 1995, Bernays started to programme in a few touring shows in the spring. In spite of the cuts that were made, it must be said a lot of money was still invested in the ReachOut programme which went from strength to strength at that time. And, in spite of all the problems, the theatre lived to fight another day, but in a different form.

The repertory system that had been the mainstay of the Everyman Theatre for the past 35 years was gone. It would probably only be missed by a few of its most devoted supporters. As Philip Bernays said, 'I don't remember that there was any great [public] protest or any campaigns to keep the rep. People just accepted it, even the Association. There was not a lot of publicity; we just got on with it. I suppose a lot of people wouldn't have noticed the difference. It was business as usual'.

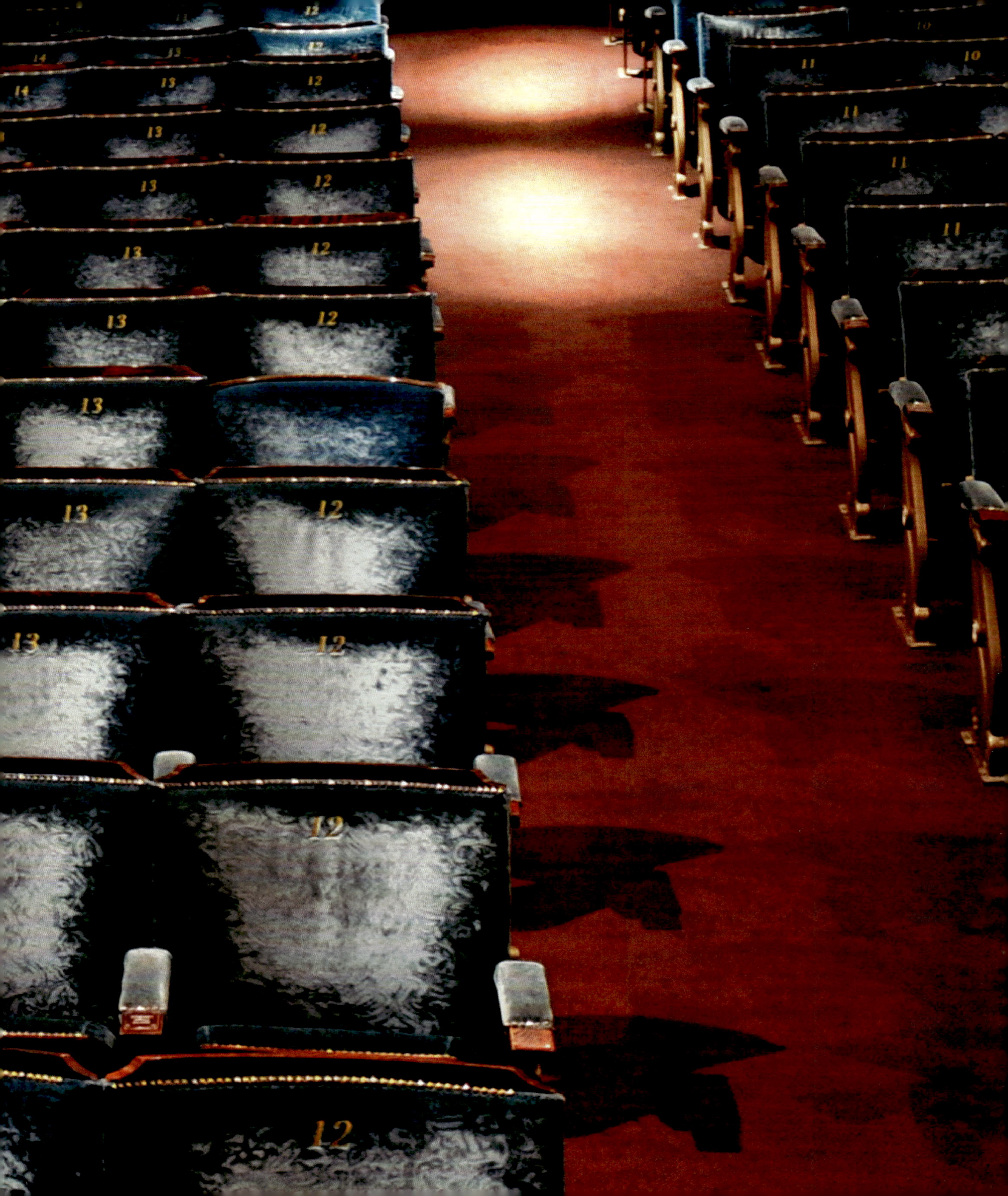

Chapter 15

For what we are about to receive
The Everyman as a receiving theatre

There had been a slow transition from rep to receiving house with some touring shows coming in at around Easter 1995. However, the first real season as a touring theatre started in the September with a visit from the cricketing comedy *Outside Edge* by Richard Harris.

In spite of initially being brought in for only three months to sort things out, Philip Bernays was to stay on for 20 months, not leaving his first stint at the theatre until the end of June 1996. Richard Hogger then became the Chief Executive until Bernays returned in 1997 to take up the post permanently.

Running a receiving house is quite different from running a rep company. With a rep company, the Artistic Director not only employs the office and front of house staff but all the actors as well. It is one big happy family. Although with a receiving house the Chief Executive selects the show, the staff of the theatre has no direct involvement with what happens on stage. Bernays did not seem to have any regrets about the demise of the rep.

'At the Everyman, the repertory company all but went bankrupt. In this day and age the finances just don't work. What there is now is much more about collaboration and co-production, to try and essentially spread the money to minimise the risks. Audiences want to see big names in every show and an old-fashioned rep company just can't do that.'

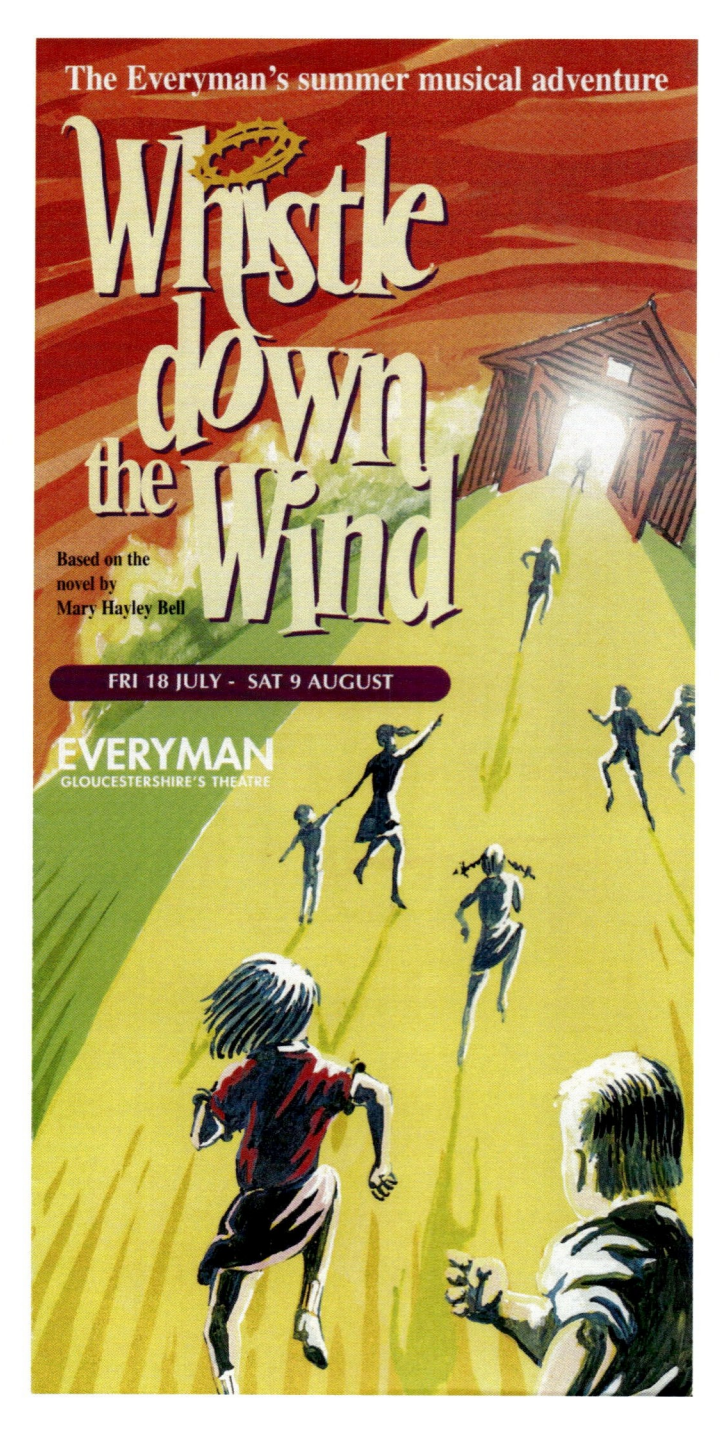

'The advantage of being a presenting theatre is that you are able to offer a much more varied and broader programme which obviously appeals to a much wider audience. You are able to present work that is, in terms of quality, of a very high standard. If we produced a show which ran for one week in this theatre, that would be the only opportunity we would have to recoup our investment. But a show that is on the road for 25 weeks has that much more time to get its money back and make a profit.'

And what about the accusations of dumming down the programming in order to maintain these high attendance levels? Was the selection of shows driven by financial motives rather than artistic integrity? 'I think we presented a broad and diverse programme. This means there were shows of greater intellectual calibre and some less so. I would say they were all good shows, none of them were boring and they were all entertaining.'

Nevertheless, Philip was happy to put on male stripper hen nights. This may have been frowned upon but he believes it added names to the theatre's database and he claims as a fact that many of the ladies, having discovered that theatre can be fun, came back to see a play.

The Everyman Youth Group had survived intact despite the end of the rep and in October 1995 they presented *Jam Tomorrow* which was produced in association with the Literature Festival that year. The play had been devised by Sue Colverd who was the new Youth and Community Director at the theatre. Sheila Mander was still there as Associate Director and Head of Education.

Apart from the Youth Group productions, the only in-house productions were, and remain, the pantomimes and occasionally studio shows. Sheila Mander, as Associate Director had responsibility for these shows. In 1997, she teamed up with composer Richard Taylor and West End designer Martin Johns to produce a spectacular adaptation of *Whistle Down the*

Wind. The show was nominated for a Barclay Theatre Award for Best Musical.

In 1997 the studio theatre was renamed. Sir Ralph had been dead fourteen years and perhaps was no longer considered relevant to modern theatre. So, The Richardson Studio ceased to exist. Philip Bernays explained the reasoning behind the change. 'We changed it to The Other Space because it was what we all actually called it around the office, because it was a nod towards or a joke around the RSC's studio and because it gave it a slightly more 'contemporary' feel'. It later became, and remains simply, The Everyman Studio Theatre.

Tudor Williams had been coming to the Everyman since the first days of rep but was quite pragmatic about the changes taking place. 'When the Richardson became The Other Space I went along to some writing workshops which Sue Colverd gave. They proved to be fascinating and we were encouraged to write in our own styles and I continued with my monologues.'

Wink Taylor is a great fan of the Studio. 'But it's just too small, you just can't make any money there. It's such a shame because I'm really fond of that space. It works very well for cabaret but we did a new musical, *Flash Garden*, there in September 2010 and had a large set which took up half the floor space. The audience seemed to be squashed up against the wall and I have to admit we felt dangerously close to them. There's no doubt about it, it's very crammed in there, but it's a brilliant space'.

Another innovation with the new regime was the introduction of the EveryKid Club, which started in 1996 and ran for about ten years. The idea was to bring mums and young children into the theatre on a Saturday morning. The shows were designed for kids from four upwards and included magic, puppets, clowns and stories.

Technically, running a touring house with the enormous variety of shows that come through can be demanding for technical staff. Bringing in the new show each week, unloading the trucks, putting up the set and arranging the lights is the responsibility of Technical Stage Manager Kieran Barker and electrician Michael E. Hall. Not always a straightforward task as Kieran explained. 'Some of the shows are quite small, just one box set which fits on to a single lorry but we have shows, *Jesus Christ Superstar* for example, using five trucks. And the big spectaculars like the ice shows present their own challenges'. Alison Greening at the stage door was aware of the problem the first

Wink Taylor
photo: Michael Hasted

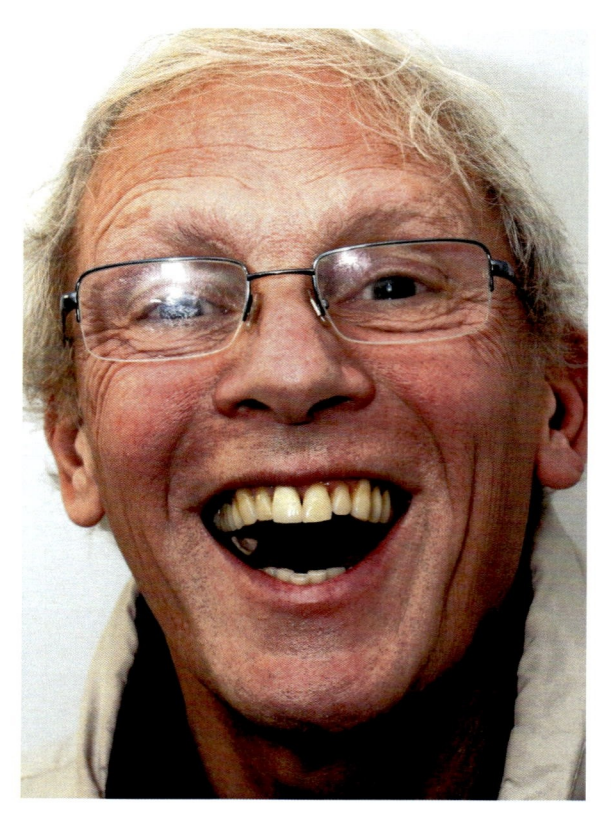

Paul Nicholas at the Everyman in 2010
photo: Michael Hasted

time the ice Russian show came. 'It takes them hours to lay the ice. They start of with a large plastic sheet and put some crushed ice on and then build up the layers with a hose over night. Well, the first time they were here, I don't know what happened but it all melted and we came in the next morning and all the under stage area was flooded, everything down there was covered in this blue slime.'

And getting the ice show out is no fun either, as Kieran knows only too well. 'Sixteen tons of ice has to be smashed up and moved out. It goes out into the yard and stays there till it melts – I've known it to take 6 weeks', he said with a rueful smile.

Sheila Mander left in 1998 and Sue Colverd took over as Artistic Director. At the time of Mander leaving, the Youth Theatre was in trouble. Philip Bernays said that the subscriptions had to double and the membership cut from 200 to 80. In an interview with *The Echo* Mander said, 'The cutbacks would kill it off within a year or two and that would be a great shame. We have an open door policy offering access to all. It's not just a numbers game; it's a question of commitment'. But the Youth Theatre survived and in fact went from strength to strength.

An Inspector Calls played a couple of times, as did another big West End hit, *Art*. Philip Bernays elaborated on this point. 'There are some shows which are perennially popular. *The Woman in Black* played Cheltenham three or four times and some of the popular dance shows, *Spirit of the Dance* for example, which we had a similar number of times'.

The Woman in Black made its first appearance at the Everyman in 2001. The play was originally commissioned and directed by Robin Herford who lives in Cheltenham. 'I moved here about the same time as *Woman* first played here. I had been based in Scarborough because of my links with Alan Ayckbourn. But it's a bit out of the way up there when I needed to travel around the country or get to airports. I needed somewhere more central.'

And it isn't just the audiences and directors that are happy to come to the Everyman. Philip Bernays again, 'The actors love it here because it's quite a small theatre so they don't have to shout so much and they have a much stronger relationship with the audience'.

Paul Nicholas played the Everyman for the first time with *The Haunting* in November 2010 and was very impressed. 'Acoustically

Robin Herford, director of
The Woman in Black
photo: Michael Hasted

it is a very good theatre. From the stage, your voice comes back very clearly; it doesn't seem weighted down by the environment. There's a sort of ambience that sends the voice out there, from an actor's point of view it an excellent stage to work on.'

Mark Hyde, who has appeared in several Everyman pantomimes, agrees. 'The acoustics are wonderful. I love the theatre, the auditorium is really intimate and you can hear a pin drop on stage at the back of the gods. When we were doing *Cinderella* at Christmas 2010 we all had these small microphones on our heads, mainly for the singing balance, but a couple of the children in the chorus had lines to say. They didn't have mics and obviously didn't have very strong voices, but everybody could hear them.'[3]

Phillip Bernays continues, 'The theatre is able to attract shows that were much bigger than is really practical. It doesn't really have the seating capacity for some of the really big productions but the producers want to bring their shows to the Everyman because they like it here. They like the Everyman because the actors like it; it's a

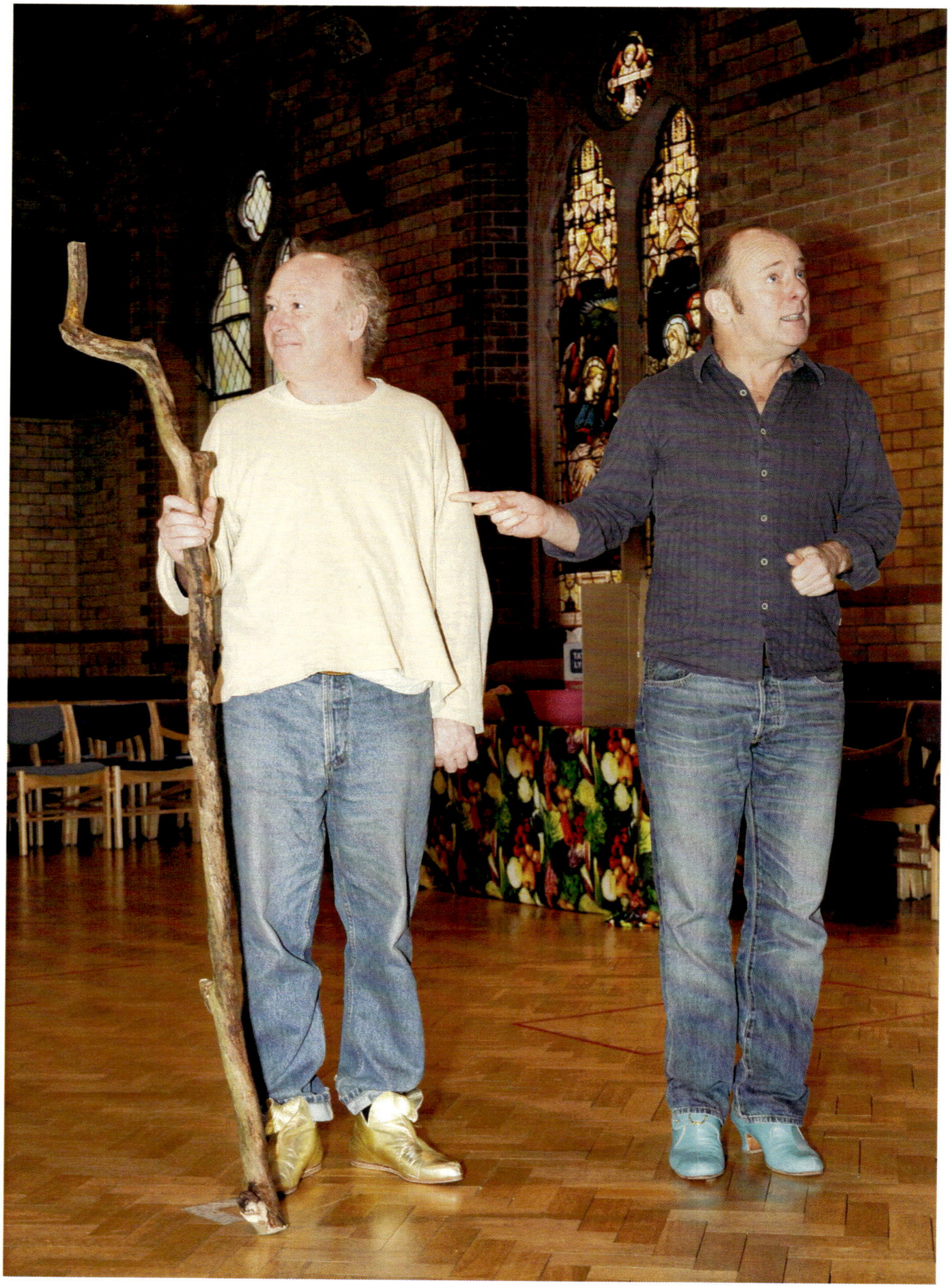

very intimate place. They like the support that is given to the shows which is absolutely second to none'.

Although opportunities to employ actors were limited to small productions in the Studio and the annual pantomime, they were not forgotten. In September 2002, The Everyman set up the Actors' Lab where local performers could meet once a week to hone, develop and maintain their skills under different practitioners. The only limitation was the size of the class and that all participants had to be Equity members.

Philip Bernays left the Everyman for pastures new at the end of 2005. 'After 10 years in Cheltenham I thought that a change would be as good as a rest and I was offered the job at the Theatre Royal, Newcastle which is a much bigger theatre which opens up lots more opportunities.'

His replacement was Geoffrey Rowe who started in February 2006. 'It was an unusual situation really. The chap who had initially been appointed decided to withdraw – after quite a long while actually – so I was called in and asked if I wanted the job with only ten day's notice. Of course I said yes.'

Until three years before his appointment in Cheltenham, Geoffrey Rowe had been with the Welsh National Opera for twelve years. 'Immediately prior to coming to the Everyman I had been working freelance, which was lucky as I was able to take up the Cheltenham job at short notice'.

A theatre manager must have his finger on all the pulses in the theatre and know what's going on back-stage, on stage and front of house. What does Geoffrey Rowe enjoy most? 'The variety I think. It's a cheery, interesting community. People work in the theatre for different reasons, but they all love the building and the institution of theatre. Everyone relates to each other and that forms a very cohesive single body of people which is good to work with.'

One of the main limitations of programming a receiving house is that you can only present what producers put on the road; it is not possible to be innovative. This can be a problem when trying to attract a new audience. 'I need to bring in quality shows that will attract a younger audience. Needless to say, audiences are the lifeblood of any theatre and ways must always be found of satisfying the current generation while encouraging the next. While not exactly fuddy-duddy, a large percentage of our audience is middle aged and middle class. To try and broaden that age range is really important', Rowe explained.

Geoffrey Rowe
photo: Michael Hasted

Opposite:

Mark Hyde and William Elliott rehearsing the 2009 pantomime
Sleeping Beauty
photo: Michael Hasted

Phil Clark directing the 2010 pantomime *Cinderella* with Zara Ramm & Amy Price in the background.
photo: Michael Hasted

Stephen Boswell returned to the theatre he grew up in, appearing in *Round the Horne* in 2005. It brought back happy memories. 'Even with the Safety Curtain down and in the working-light's jaundiced glare, I could still picture the old stage, smell the scent of magic that still lingered on the barren boards and in the dusty wings. It was in the smell of size that I remembered; that and the pigeons nesting in the roof of the old dressing-rooms.'

In spite of the broad diversity of shows passing through the Everyman over the years, it has almost managed to maintain a tiny element, the smallest hint of rep. The pantomime in recent years has used more or less the same company and director.

Phil Clark directed his first pantomime in Cheltenham in 2006 and was to return often in the following years. He wanted to build a group of regulars. 'I'm very keen to have actors that the audience can become familiar with, rather like the old rep companies. For several years I've used Mark Hyde, Zara Ramm and Willie Elliott as the dame for my Everyman pantomimes.'

Clark's approach to pantomime has always been traditional. He refuses to allow them to become vehicles to revitalise the career of some aging soap-star or punch-drunk boxer. 'I've got nothing against soap stars but I like to use good, solid performers. The audiences like that and develop an involvement over the years. I'm not really interested in using star names, the culture and traditions of pantomime are more important and I think the kids appreciate that.'

Clark's pantomimes are truly traditional with all the glamour and magic that that entails. But what has been lacking in all pantomimes in recent years is the speciality acts. In the old days you would always get the Broker's Men, for example, who would do a juggling act in the second half or a ventriloquist would do a few minutes. You rarely get that any more. Phil agrees. 'I think that reflects what's happened in British entertainment over the years and the demise of variety. The nearest we get to it is the *X Factor* or *Britain's Got Talent*.'

Luckily, that's not entirely true. Cheltenham based Wink Taylor and his partner Wendy Abrahams still work in variety and have appeared in several pantomimes at the Everyman. They were in Phil Clark's 2010 production of *Cinderella* with Wink playing Buttons and Wendy as Dandini.

Wink was able to demonstrate some of his many talents in the show; he juggled, rode his unicycle and did an illusion but it was his alter ego, Theo the Mouse, that was his real speciality act. 'Although I'm only just in my forties I'm a traditional variety entertainer. Wendy and I do pantomime for two or three months, then do summer season at the seaside.'

Paul Milton, who was appointed the Everyman's Artistic Director after three years as director of ReachOut, tried to gather together a group of actors, very often local, for his productions in the Studio. About half the shows that he puts on there are home grown. 'That's right, there are lots a small, professional theatre companies around here, a lot of them around Stroud. In the old days most actors lived in London and were reluctant to come out to the provinces, fearing they'd miss something. Now lots of actors are based regionally and it's not a problem. Another reason I like to use local actors is that I don't have to pay them £125 a week subsistence.

'One of my real aims is to launch a show in the Studio and take it to other theatres so that audiences outside Gloucestershire get to see

Paul Milton
photo: Michael Hasted

Stephen Boswell
photo: Scott Rylander

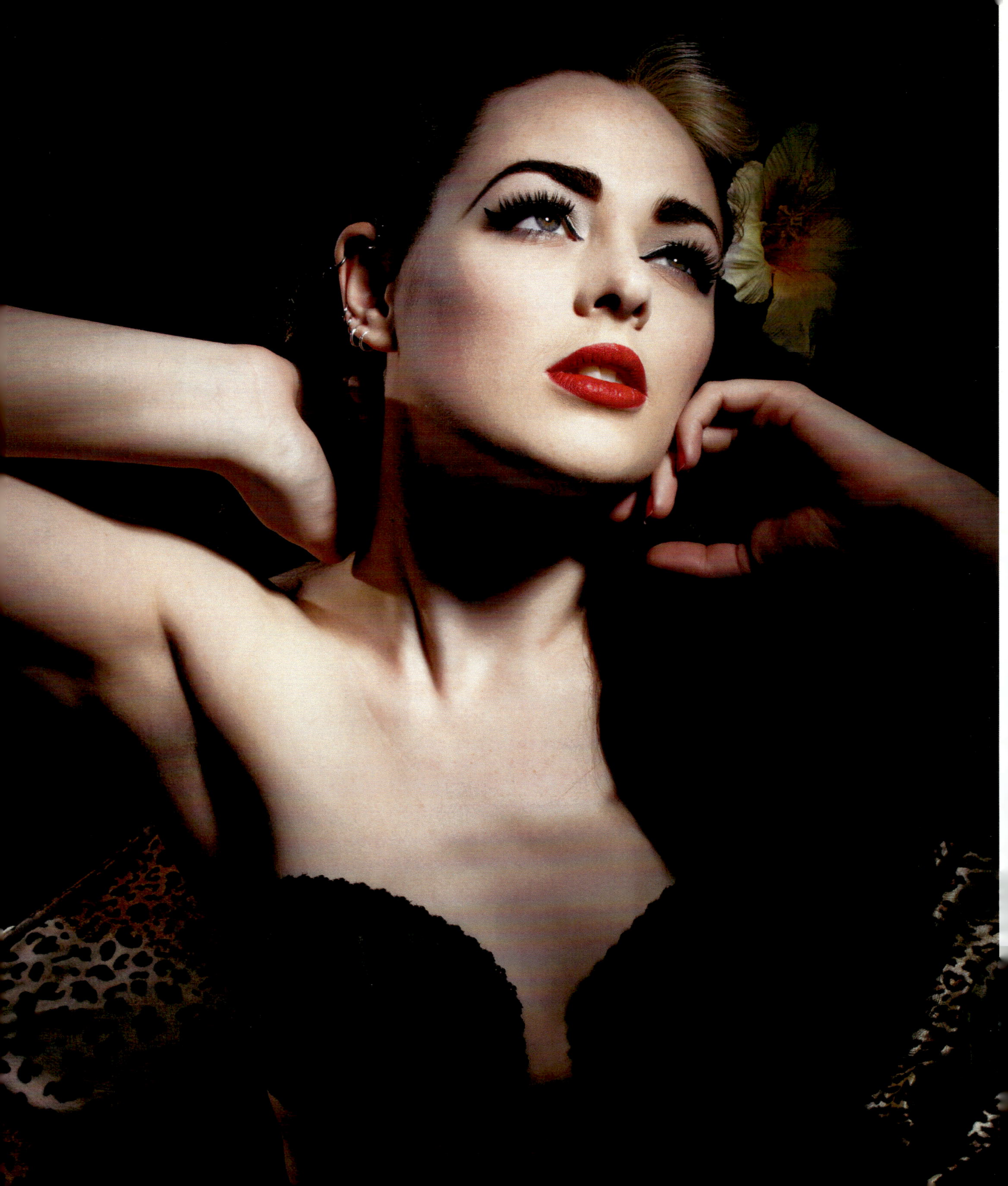

that the Everyman is not just a receiving house. We have a pool of actors that we tend to use and that almost has the feel of a mini rep company. The old rep system that I grew up in has all but gone, but that's what I'd like to create in the Studio; to have three or four actors doing a series of different shows spread over a few weeks'.

Paul regrets the passing of the old rep system because it inspired a great loyalty in the audience. 'That's exactly what I'm after in the Studio. A loyal audience that will come and see really good work and then be prepared to take a risk on a play that they don't know. It's got to be about risk. The actors take risks, the director takes risks and we want to encourage the audience to take risks. The tickets cost well under half of the main house, so what have they got to lose?'

'I'd love to get a bit of weight in there. I can understand that during a recession people want cheering up but you have to be careful or you end up with just lightweight stuff and nothing else. What I'm trying to do in the Studio is to mix intimate, light-weight revue type theatre with some new writing and ideas. In fact the last show we put on before the theatre closed for restoration in April 2011 was a brand new revue called *Final Daze* written for us by Michael Hasted who had worked at the Everyman in the very early days of rep. Finding good stuff to put on can be a bit of a slog sometimes, but you must try and get that balance.'

The problem with provincial studio theatres is that, to a certain extent, they get the same audience that goes to the main house; it's difficult in a provincial town to find a completely new and different audience that will be keen to embrace new and experimental theatre. Milton produces about three or four shows a year in the studio but the lack of space is a chronic problem. 'No show we put on there can ever pay for itself. With only 50 or sixty seats and a five night run, it can't. So, the problem is always funding. I have to pay the actors Equity minimum which, with National Insurance, travel expenses, holiday pay and all the rest, can come to the best part of £500 a week. So you don't need a calculator to work out that selling 250 or 300 seats for a show at £7.50 each isn't going to cover it'.

One show that was always very successful in the Studio was the burlesque spectacle presented by Cheltenham based exotic dancer, Missy Malone. One might feel that burlesque would be a little out of place in the Everyman, but Missy felt quite at home there. But is the show titillation or is it theatre? She is in no doubt at all. 'Oh, theatre, absolutely. It's all to do with glamour, costume choice and there is even some characterisation in the comedy routines. I have about twelve routines and in half of them I hardly remove anything, certainly a lot less than people are expecting.' After Missy's success, a bigger touring Burlesque show appeared in the main house in October 2011.

Opposite:

Burlesque star Missy Malone
photo: Miss Rain Photography

A damaged cherub on the front of one
of the boxes, prior to restoration in 2011
photo: Michael Hasted

Chapter 16

The cherubs smile again
The Everyman is restored to its former glory

It was once said of Marcel Duchamp, the father of Dada, the precursor of Surrealism, that his work was, to paraphrase, like 'a knife with a new handle, the blade of which has also been replaced'.

Restoring old buildings can be rather like that. When starting work it is often difficult to know which features are original and which have been added on or changed later. The situation is exacerbated if there isn't a lot of information available from the original build.

This was the dilemma facing the Everyman Theatre leading up to its major restoration in 2011. The theatre's chief executive, Geoffrey Rowe, explained the problem before work started. 'Although we are making every effort, we cannot, in reality, go back to 1891 when the theatre first opened. It will probably be more like 1931; that's when they really started make major alterations and changed the way the building looked. There are only very sketchy plans of the original theatre. The detailed plans and Matcham's drawings disappeared some time ago.

'However, there is a very full description of the original theatre's décor from the newspapers and journals of the time. They listed and described everything in great detail and gave all the colours, but that's about all we've got. But that, in itself, can cause problems. When they describe a colour as 'coral' what exactly does that mean? There are a dozen shades that could be described as 'coral'.'

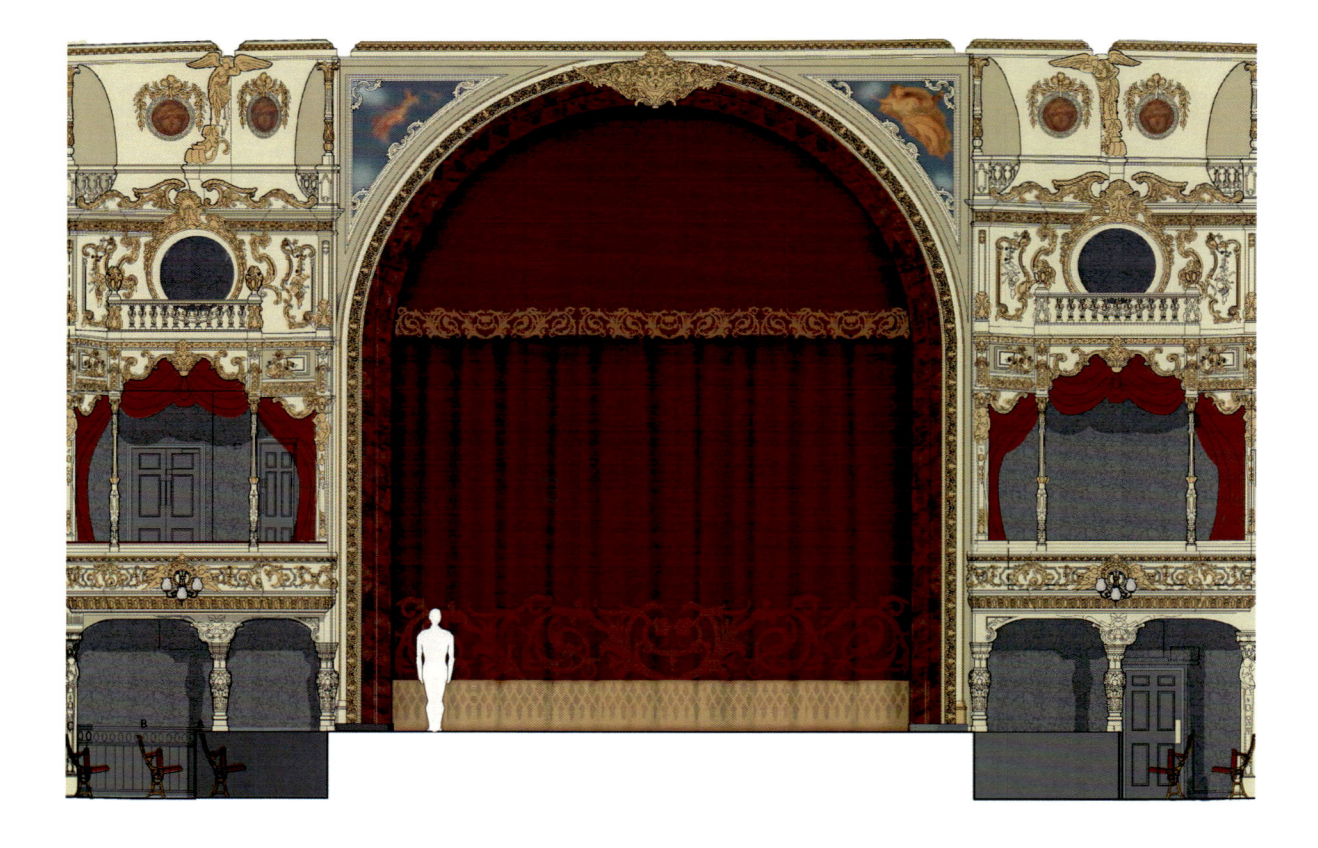

both pages: Original drawings for the restoration by London architects Foster Wilson
Courtesy of and copyright Foster Wilson Architects 2010

The life and soul of any old building lies not only in its history but in the rich layers of patina that have built up over the years. However, patina is often a polite way of describing dirt and grime and consequently there can be a very fine line between charming and tatty, one that Geoffrey Rowe was very aware of. 'I think there is a sentimental reaction by everyone who is interested in the theatre to prevent lovely old buildings like this from disintegrating.'

'But apart from the slightly sentimental indulgence which prompted us to press on and raise money and make plans, there was a serious commercial aspect involved in the restoration as well. No matter how affectionate people feel towards their local theatre, a lack of comfort, a lack of style and the inevitable shabbiness will eventually start alienating people. I think eventually that lack of comfort would have started a cycle of decline which could have brought this theatre down. It was therefore important, from a commercial standpoint, to sustain the theatre as a viable public building and to ensure that it continued to thrive physically as well as intellectually.'

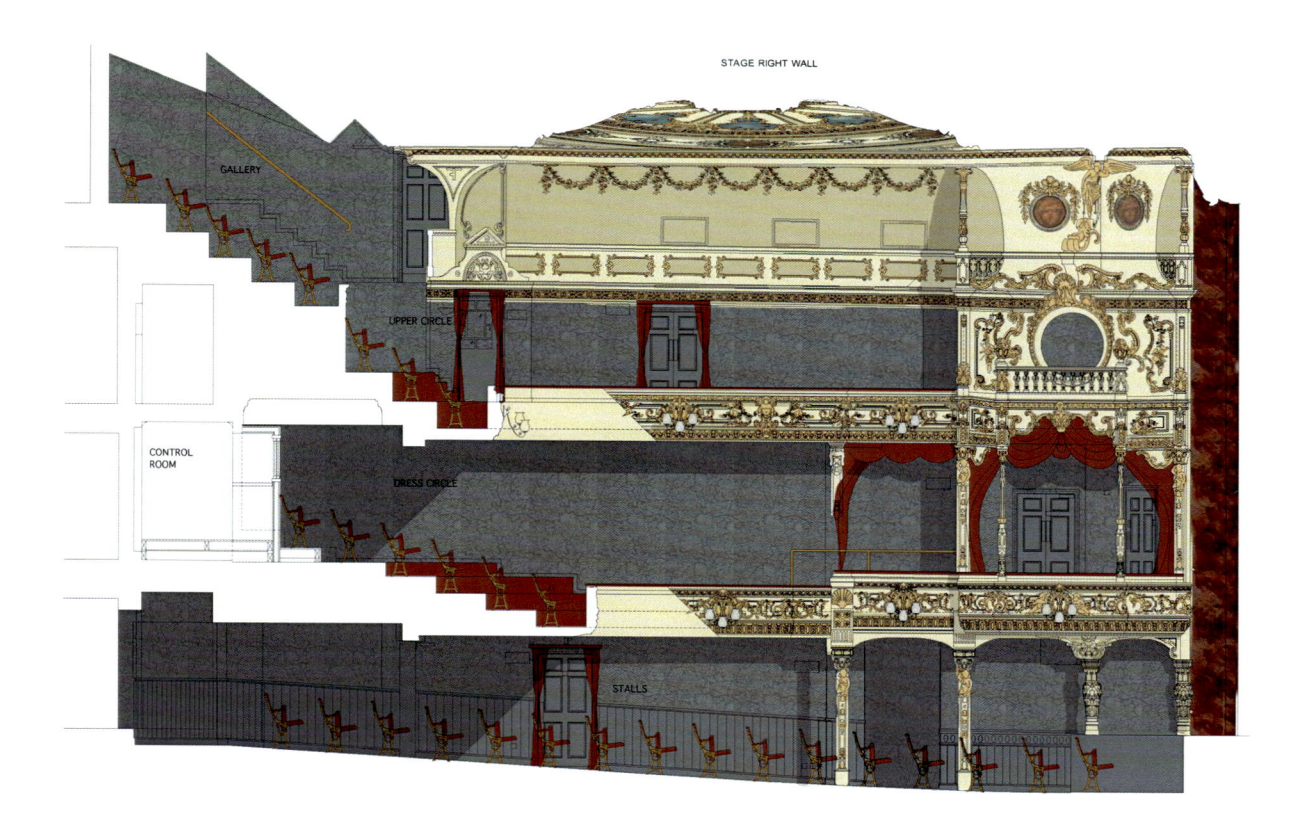

The need for a restoration had been clear for some time and the replacement of the seats and installation of air conditioning ductwork in 2000/1 was supposed to be the first of a number of stages. In 2004/5, plans moved forward with the appointment of an architect and the commissioning of a heritage survey, but the plans floundered when the Lottery Board turned down the Everyman's draft application at stage one. There were more delays caused by the departure of Philip Bernays in 2005.

However, things began to look up in 2006 when the Everyman received a VAT refund of over £500,000 due to an earlier EEC ruling. This enabled the theatre to pay for the early design and survey stages and to ask for matched funding from the Heritage Lottery and the Cheltenham Borough Council, both of whom came through with grants and loans.

Although the front of house received a fairly substantial make over, it was the auditorium where most of the work took place. Over the years, the theatre has gone through many changes; it was probably the auditorium that received the least attention. The 2011 restoration was almost certainly the most thorough and complete in the theatre's long history.

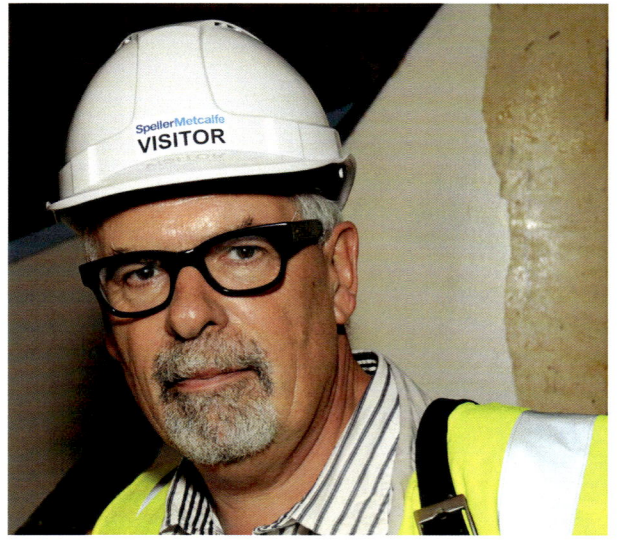

Geoffrey Rowe explained what that entailed. 'A lot of the plasterwork had got chipped or damaged over the years and many of the cherubs had arms and legs missing. The house lights had always been very harsh and didn't really show off the décor to its best advantage so all that was dealt with. Additionally, all the old and rather makeshift scaffolding rigs which supported the lights and speakers in a haphazard way were replaced and made much more discreet or concealed altogether. Ugly cables for lighting and sound snaked around the walls and pillars and needed to be hidden away. There are brand new, much more comfortable seats in the stalls and dress circle which we have kept in the original style. Many of the seats that had been here before were cinema seats and were set at a completely different angle to theatre seats. The wrought-iron end-panels of the rows were specially designed for us and, of course, the new upholstery and carpets were all colour coordinated to match the overall scheme.

'We made great efforts to be sympathetic to what was already here. We received listed building consent only on the condition that we met certain standards. There were lots of preliminary drawings and sketches and colour samples and all that sort of thing, but there are always compromises, you can never go back to exactly as it was,' Rowe explained.

The company engaged to undertake the restoration was Foster Wilson Architects of London who specialise in all sorts of theatre work including new-build. Tim Foster explained his involvement. 'My practice was selected in February 2008 to design and manage the project. Arriving at a final package of works was the subject of much discussion, in which the design team, together with The Everyman and the conservation authorities, sought to find the right balance between historical accuracy, modern operational and commercial needs and a constrained budget.'

After more than ten years of planning, meetings, submissions, fund raising and a *Conservation Plan* put together by the specialist company Theatre*Search* in 2005, work finally got under way on site in May 2011. Tim Foster described the sequence of events, 'The first thing that happened was that we removed all the seats and had to repair the floor in the stalls before the scaffolding went up'.

When everything was clear, the entire auditorium was filled with scaffolding and not one nook, cranny or cherub was left unprodded, uncleaned or unpainted. Unsightly water damage that had remained on the ceiling from the backstage roof fire in the eighties was repaired and repainted.

The only actual structural work in the auditorium involved the two stage boxes. When the pillars supporting the dress circle were removed in the 1930s they also removed the pillars supporting the boxes. This caused problems as Tim Foster explained. 'The removal of the pillars under the boxes was quite unnecessary as the columns were not obstructing sight-lines. Consequently the boxes started to sag and had to be propped up with girders and unsightly diagonal tie-

above: Part of the original *scagliola* of the proscenium arch revealed at the start of restoration

opposite top: The first week of the restoration project – clearing the decks

opposite bottom: Project architect, Tim Foster

All photos Michael Hasted

Chapter 16   The cherubs smile again

bars which made them unusable. We re-installed the columns which gave them all the support they needed so all the other paraphernalia could be removed and they could be re-commissioned. The stage boxes in theatres of this period play a crucial role in visually linking the auditorium galleries to the proscenium and they should properly be populated by members of the audience.'

The proscenium was finally restored to its former glory after layers of paint that had built up over the decades were removed. The original *faux marble* arch provided guidance that determined the colour scheme. Tim Foster again, 'From the outset our approach was to seek to interpret the 1891 colours rather than to stick too rigidly to the findings of our scientific reports. The paint analysis provided us with exact shades but we made these colours several tones darker than the originals. We felt this was an important adjustment as the original colours would have been viewed under gaslight or low levels of electric light, rather than the higher brightness levels of modern lighting.

'There was no clear evidence to suggest what colour the side and rear walls were so we sought an interpretation to contrast with the cream and tan decorative plaster and the deep red fabrics. We decided to use a blue/grey decorative wallpaper, complementing the restored proscenium and the sky blue panels in the dome. This also reinforced the new house lighting scheme which highlights the balcony fronts, side boxes and dome while recessing the side and rear walls. The wallpaper, which was specially made, is based on a fragment recovered from the Everyman but in a new colourway to suit the new scheme'.

Luckily, specialist craftsmen are still available to work on the fibrous plasterwork and all the other original features, but Foster considers the preparatory work was the most important. 'The most challenging part of the work was done beforehand, all the research that had to be done – getting the colour schemes right, getting the fittings right. We had some new seating made but restored others and we had new carpets based on Matcham originals. The main curtain and other drapes were replaced. Matcham considered this 'soft architecture' as important as any other part of the décor.

'One particular challenge in this sort of restoration is managing the technical installations. Of course, in the original building there were no provisions made for modern lighting and sound systems so finding ways of solving those problems in a way which is sympathetic to the building but also functions on a technical level can be difficult.

'We also changed the stalls seating layout to eliminate the centre gangway and improve the row spacing. This caused some complaints from patrons who like to have aisle seats in the centre but I think the general improvement in comfort levels and the elimination of the gap

The SpellerMetcalfe team work out a plan of action. May 2011

Clearly in need of some tender loving care. One of the pillars and some unsightly cables up the centre of the stalls, which actors dislike, justified the change.'

The main building contactor for the restoration was SpellerMetcalfe of Gloucester. From the beginning, Andy Metcalfe was aware of the challenges. 'It involved a great deal of specialist work, including fibrous plaster work, specialist decoration and art restoration, as well as complex technical issues. It was an amazing project and one we were delighted to be involved in.'

Although the main important work was done in the auditorium, substantial changes and improvements were also made in the front of house areas. The whole of the FOH was gutted, the toilets were ripped out, walls knocked down and the old curved staircase from the cafe to the bar was replaced.

Specialist plasterers repairing the Everyman's intricate and ornate ceiling. May 2011
all photos: Michael Hasted

Since its opening in 1891, Cheltenham's theatre has weathered many storms and come through many financial crises. It withstood onslaught, first from films and then from television which led to its darkest hour in 1959 when its ignominious closure seemed unavoidable. But out of that despair, The Everyman rose like a phoenix to enter what was possibly the theatre's greatest and most rewarding decades of its long and illustrious life.

People still talk of the rep companies and reminisce about the actors that graced the theatre's stage. They were not famous or stars of the small screen but nor were they just passing through for a week. They belonged to the theatre and the theatre belonged to them. They were committed to its success and survival. A repertory company encourages and rewards loyalty and, to a certain extent, an audience knows what to expect – even though that can sometimes seem unexciting and parochial compared with the large, big budgets touring shows.

Since 1995 the theatre has played host to some of the biggest names and most exciting shows that toured the country. It has presented straight plays, lavish musicals, ice shows and pantomimes; all of a quality that was never possible with the chronically under-funded and under-resourced rep system.

The newly restored Everyman Theatre re-opened on 23rd September 2011 with a spectacular show by the indomitable Ken Dodd. On

Painting of the Everyman's beautiful domed celing nearing completion, June 2011
photo: Michael Hasted

Sunday 2nd October, a day of celebrations took place in Regent Street to commemorate, not only the re-opening but also the theatre's one hundred and twentieth anniversary. The festivities culminated in an evening of Victorian entertainment hosted by actor Robert Powell.

The story of the Everyman Theatre is typical of many theatres around Great Britain. With the demise of the old rep system theatres have had to adapt. Those which failed to do so, rarely survived.

The Everyman Theatre in Cheltenham's Regent Street has not only survived all the crisis that began in the mid-fifties and which continued for another forty years, but it has flourished.

The Everyman has introduced a wide variety of shows to a wide variety of people. It has created an audience where there often wasn't one before. It has not been afraid to be popular nor ashamed to be traditional.

It truly could be said to be the provider of genuine, all-round entertainment – a theatre for all seasons.

Acknowledgements

Steven Berkoff; Terry Aubrey; everyone at the Everyman Theatre, especially Francesca Goddard and Jackie McKenzie in the Press Office, Paul Milton, John Whitehead, Roger Hendry and of course Geoffrey Rowe; Josephine Tewson; William Gaunt; David Gilmore; Stephen Boswell; Robert Whelan; Ian Mullins; Tim Foster; Malcolm Farquhar; Donald Crosby; Martin Houghton; Nettie Edwards; Sheila Mander; Roger Nicholls; Philip Bernays; Sally Self, Joyce Cummings and Roger Beacham of The Cheltenham Local History Society; Sue Rowbotham and Jill Waller; Rachel Roberts at the Ladies' College; The Director of GCHQ; Kath Boothman; Ann-Rachael Harwood, Helen Brown and Anna Stanway at the Cheltenham Museum and Art Gallery; Matthew Lloyd of the Arthur Lloyd website; Kate Dunn for permission to use extracts from *Exit Through the Fireplace*; Jill Barlow, archivist at Cheltenham College; Stephen Blake; Hilary Jennings; Rodney Stoneman; Edward Bottle; Tony Jones; Jeremy Mills, Hazel Goodes, Sarah Whitham, the editorial team and everyone at Jeremy Mills Publishing Ltd. And, of course, everyone else who talked to me, supplied material, information or stories for this history. Whilst every effort was made to attribute pictures used in this book there were, of course, pictures whose origins have been lost in the mists of time. We acknowledge their use and apologise for being unable to credit them.

Notes

CLHS = Cheltenham Local History Society

Chapter 1
[1] *CLHS Journal 20* article by Jill Waller & Vic Cole p.18
[2] *Cirencester Flying Post* 6th August 1744
[3] *The Gloucester Journal* July 1758
[4] *Georgian Cheltenham* Edith Humhris & Captain E.C. Willoughby. Publ. 1928
[5] *Georgian Cheltenham* Edith Humhris & Captain E.C. Willoughby. Publ. 1928
[6] *Cheltenham; A History* by Rowbotham & Waller. Phillimore Press
[7] *Georgian Cheltenham* Edith Humhris & Captain E.C. Willoughby. Publ. 1928
[8] *Georgian Cheltenham* Edith Humhris & Captain E.C. Willoughby. Publ. 1928
[9] *Cheltenham; A History* by Rowbotham & Waller. Phillimore Press p.77
[10] *CLHS Journal 12* article by Leslie Burgess p.19
[11] *CLHS Journal 12* article by Leslie Burgess p.20
[12] *CLHS Journal 21* article by Leslie Burgess p.54
[13] *CLHS Journal 8* article p.26
[14] *A Short History of the First Cheltenham Spa at Bayshill* by Andrea Jones, Cheltenham Ladies College 1988
[15] *CLHS Journal 12* article by Roger Beacham p.22

Chapter 2
[1] *The Cheltenham Examiner* 23rd April 1890 p.4
[2] *Drama in Gloucestershire*, Theodore Hannam-Clark, 1928
[3] *The Gloucestershire Echo* 19th September 1891
[4] *The Cheltenham Examiner* 23rd April 1890 p.8
[5] *The Stage* 3rd June 1948
[6] *The Cheltenham Examiner* 23rd September 1891 p.8

Chapter 3
[1] Introduction by David Butler to *The Days That I Knew* by L. Langtry. Futura 1978
[2] *The Cheltenham Examiner* 7th October 1891
[3] *The Era* 3rd October 1891 p.11
[4] *CLHS Journal 25* Article by Roger Beacham
[5] Forward to *McCarthy, Lillah Myself and my Friends*, 1933
[6] Anthony Camp, *Royal Mistresses and Bastards: Fact & Fiction 1714-1936* (London, 2007) p.365
[7] *The Cheltenham Looker-On* 3rd October 1891 *Sayings & Doings of Cheltenham*
[7] *CLHS Journal 8* article p.26
[9] *The Cheltenham Examiner* 1892

Chapter 4
[1] *The Stage* 25th October 1900
[2] www.arthurlloyd.co.uk
[3] *The Stage* 8th May 1913

Chapter 5
[1] *The Stage* 14th April 1921 p.20
[2] *The Gloucestershire Echo* 25th August 1925 p.1
[3] *The Gloucestershire Echo* 27th September 1929 p.1
[4] *The Gloucestershire Echo* 27th September 1929 p.1
[5] *The Gloucestershire Echo* 24th September 1929 p.5
[6] *CLHS Journal 19* article by Roger Beacham pp.31-39
[7] *The Straits Times*, Singapore September 1929 p.12
[8] *The Stage* 28th January 1932 p.12
[9] *CLHS Journal 12* article by Roger Beacham pp. 22-26
[10] *The Stage* 26th November 1931 p.13
[11] *The Stage* 28th January 1932 p.12
[12] *CLHS Journal 19* article by Roger Beacham pp.31-39
[13] *The Gloucestershire Echo* 2nd August 1934 p.6
[14] *The Gloucestershire Echo* 4th December 1935
[15] *CLHS Journal 12* article by Roger Beacham pp. 22-26
[16] *The Stage* 24th January 1935 p.9
[17] *The Stage* 10th May 1939

Chapter 6
[1] *The Stage* 28th September 1939
[2] *The Stage* 2nd January 1941 p.12
[3] *The Stage* 23rd April 1942

Chapter 7
[1] *The Stage* 3rd January 1946 p.5
[2] *The Gloucestershire Echo* 1st November 1955
[3] *The Gloucestershire Echo* 1st November 1955
[4] *The Gloucestershire Echo* 1st November 1955
[5] *The Stage* 10th November 1955 p.8
[6] *The Gloucestershire Echo* 1st November 1955
[7] *The Stage* 1st August 1957

⁸ *The Stage* 28th May 1959
⁹ President of the ETA's report, 22nd November 1962
¹⁰ Notes in tenth anniversary programme 28th February 1970

Chapter 8
¹ *Gloucestershire Echo*, 19th June 1959
² *Gloucestershire Echo*, 29th October 1959
³ *Bristol Evening Post*, 7th December 1959
⁴ *Gloucestershire Echo*, 29th October 1959
⁵ *Speaking Volumes, A History of the Cheltenham Festival of Literature*. 1999 Sutton Publishing
⁶ *The Stage*, 3rd November 1960
⁷ Rae Hammond writing in programme notes 7th January 1971

Chapter 9
¹ *Gloucestershire Echo* 29th October 1959
² *ETA Newsletter* No. 37 August 1966

Chapter 10
¹ *The Stage* 28th September 1961
² *The Stage* 4th June 1964 p.9
³ *The Stage* 20th December 1967 p.16
⁴ Theatre programme notes 2nd September 1969
⁵ *The Stage* 17th September 1970

Chapter 11
¹ *The Stage* 15th April 1971
² *The Stage* 24 January 1974 p.23
³ *Exit Through the Fireplace* by Kate Dunn. John Murray 1998 p.17
⁴ Theatre programme notes 7th January 1971
⁵ *The Stage* 30th September 1982 p.2

Chapter 14
¹ *The Stage* 20th November 1986 p.2
² Theatre programme notes 20th February 1986
³ *The Stage* 20th March 1986 p.11
⁴ Programme notes
⁵ *The Stage* 25th April 1991 p.2
⁶ Theatre programme notes February 1993
⁷ *The Stage* 9th March 1995. p.2
⁸ *The Stage* 23rd March 1995 p.4

Chapter 15
¹ *The Gloucestershire Echo* 16th February 1998 piece by Clare Parrack p. 9

Managers, Artistic Directors, Chairmen and CEOs

General Managers of the Opera House
Charles Chappell	(1891–1899)
George Abel	(1899–1900)
H. Oswald Redford	(1900–1924)
Wilfred Simpson	(1925–1955)
Peter Carpenter	(1955–1957)
Frank Maddox	(1957–1959)

Artistic Directors, Everyman repertory companies
Peter Powell	(May 1960–Feb 1961)
David Giles	(Mar 1961–June 1961)
Ian Mullins	(Sept 1961–May 1968)
Michael Ashton	(May 1968–Nov 1970)
Rae Hammond (acting)	(Nov 1970–May 1971)
Malcolm Farquhar	(May 1971–Feb 1983)
John Doyle	(July 1985–Aug 1989)
Martin Houghton	(Sept 1989–Jan 1995)

General Managers of the repertory theatre
William Bland Wood	(1960–1961)
John Ridley	(1961–1965)
Rae Hammond	(1965–1982)
John Hurt	(1982–1986)
Margaret Jones	(1986–1987)
Douglas Fraser	(1987–1990)
Bubble Lodge (later CEO)	(1990–1995)

Chairmen of the Board of Directors
Noel Newman	(1960–1970)
John Bradby	(1970–1972)
William G. Poeton	(1973–1977)
Christopher Powell	(1977–1991)
Hugh Raymond	(1991–1997)
Darryl Whitehead	(1997–1998)
Edward Gillespie	(1998–2005)
Clive Thomas	(2005–

Chief Executives of the receiving theatre
Philip Bernays	(1995–1996)
Roger Hogger	(1996–1997)
Philip Bernays	(1997–2005)
Geoffrey Rowe	(2006–

Old map of central Cheltenham showing locations of theatres etc.

Based on a Ward Lock *RED GUIDE* map c. 1930s

1. Coffee House Yard Theatre
2. The original Theatre Royal
3. The second Theatre Royal
4. The Assembly Rooms
5. Sadlers Wells Puppet theatre
6. The Royal Old Well
7. The Winter Gardens
8. Montpellier Gardens
9. The Opera House/Everyman
10. The Repertory Theatre
11. The Hippodrome/Coliseum

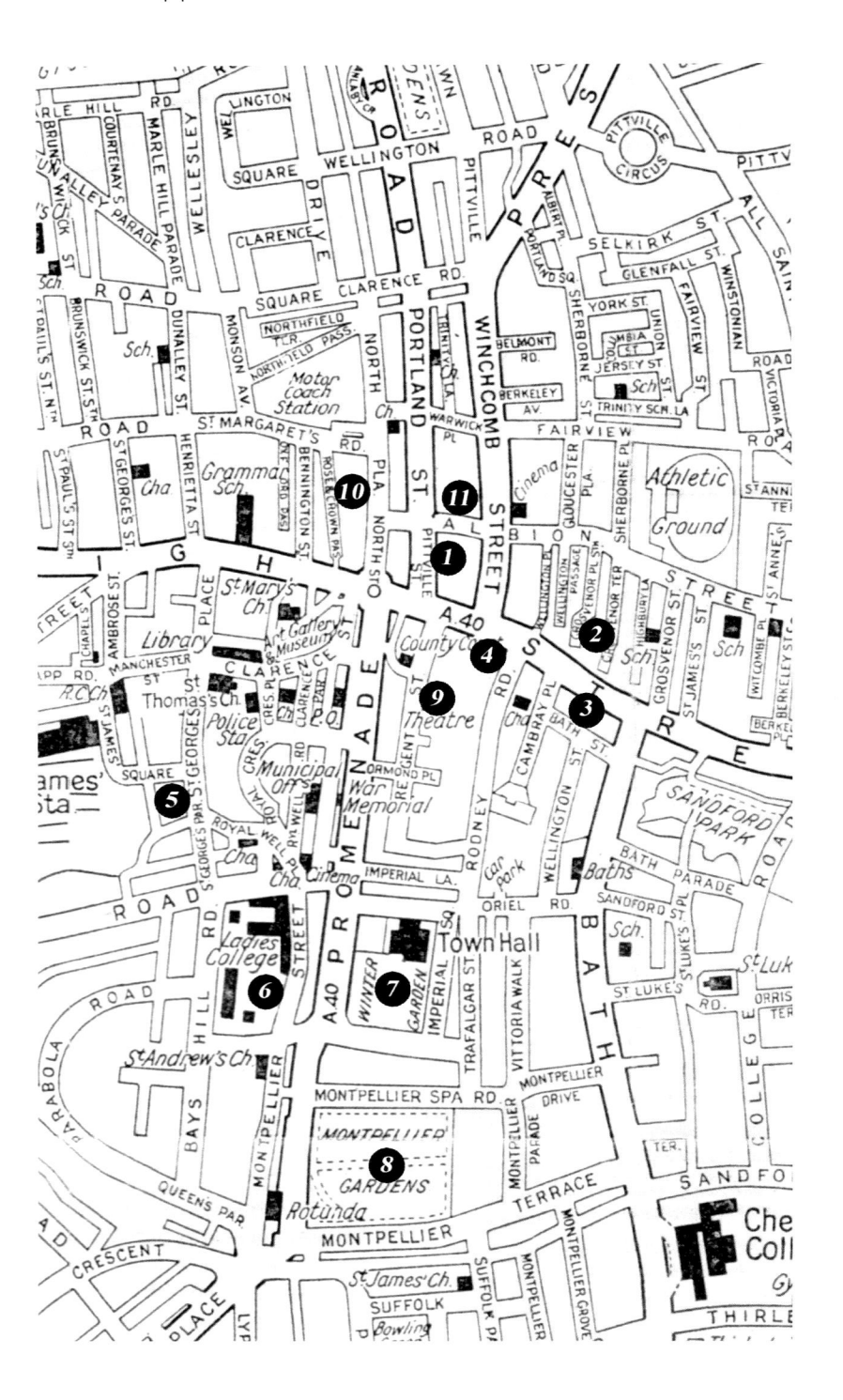

Index

A

Abel, George 29
Abrahams, Wendy 161
Action Theatre 107
Actors' Lab 159
Adrian, Max 56
Agg, Colonel 13
Ailesbury, Lord 3
air-raids 47, 53, 73
Albert Hall 43
Albion Street *31*, 32, 33
Alexandra Theatre, Birmingham 45
Andree, Rosemary 56, 57
Andrews, Ross 146
Arts Council 85, 101, 102, 112, 113, 115, 117, 131, 148, 149, 150
Arts Theatre, Cambridge 73
Ashby, Harvey 89, 96
Ash, John Gordon 64, 65, 67
Ashton, Michael 102, 103, ***103***, 105, 106, 112
Assembly Rooms 6, 7, ***8***, 11, 13, 22, 31, 32
As You Like It 3, 25, 96
Austen, Jane 5

B

Bagshot de la Bere, Reverend John 43
Bailey, Iris 63, 120
Baird, George Alexander 25, 26, ***26***
Barker, Harley Granville 23
Barker, Kieran 129, 155, 156
Barrett, Roger 128
Barter, Nicholas 80, 83
Barter, Sylvia 83
Barter-Spencer *see* Barter

Bath Road 9, 87
Bath Street 5
Bayshill 26
Bayshill Road 7
Beard, H.G. 38, 43
Beechwood Arcade 38
Belgrade Theatre, Coventry 73, 79
Bellman & Ivey 18
Benson, Frank 22
Berkeley Castle 5
Berkeley, Colonel 5, 7
Berkoff, Steven vii, 75-77, ***75***
Bernays, Philip 147-151, ***150***, 153-7, 159, 167
Bernhardt, Sarah 23
Beryl, Pat 55
Big Classical 70, ***70***
Biggs, Lt. Colonel C. W. 62
Binns, Jonas 17, ***17***, 18
Birmingham Rep 98
Black, Alan 97
Blackpool 15
Black, Alan 97
Bland Wood, Bill 120
Bletchley Park 81, 82
Blithe Spirit 98
Blower, Ronald and George 37, 38
Bolt, Robert 64, 90
Borowski, Caroline 125
Boswell, Stephen 57, 67, 74, 93, 120, ***120***, 160, ***161***
Bradby, Edward 103
Bridgeman family, Devon 14
Bristol 3, 42
Bristol Hippodrome 15
Bristol Old Vic 55, 70
Britton, Tony ***110***, 111
Brocket, Peter 120
Brooker, Rebecca 5

Burchell, Rex 43, 44, 45, ***45***
Burne, Rosamund ***106***
Burton, Richard 56, 127
Byron, Lord 5

C

Cabbages and Kings 97
Cambray 5
Carpenter, Peter 63
Carr, Anne 91, ***91***
Caunter, Tony 145
Cavendish House 65, 67, 91
Chappell, Charles 14, 24, 27, 29
Charlton Kings 35, 125
Cheltenham College 70
Cheltenham Council 41, 43, 47, 62, 64, 68, 69, 89, 115, 127, 136, 167
Cheltenham Grammar School 82, 83, 91, 146, 147, 150
Cheltenham Literature Festival 73, 102, 141, 154
Cheltenham Theatre Association 67, 68, 70
Chester, Charlie 53
Cider With Rosie 113
Cinema House Ltd. 41
Cinema at the Opera House 41
Cirencester 3, 19, 51
Clarke, Richard 2
Clark, Phil 160, ***160***, 161
Cleeve Hill 1, 52, 74, 99
Close, Rev. Francis 5, 7, 8
CODS 57, 65, 87, ***87***
Coffee House Lane 2
Coffee House Yard Theatre 2
Coliseum 33, 38, 39, 43, ***43***
Coliseum Theatre, London 15
Colosseum, Bath Road 9
Colverd, Sue 154-156

Compton, Ellen 43
Compton, Fay 43
Compton, Jean 44
Connections 140
Connor, Kenneth 55
Cooke, George 10
Coronation Street 59, 95
C.O.R.T. 96
Courtneidge, Cicely *52*, 109
Crazy Gang 51, 53
Croker-King, Lt. Colonel 14
Crosby, Donald 108, *108*, 114, 115, 116, 128, 136
Croswell, Chris 141

D

Dankworth, Jacqueline 138
Dankworth, John 138
Davies, Margaret 57, 67-69, *69*, 74, 75, 106
Davies, Rupert 55
Davies, Windsor 76
Denyer, Peter 111, 128
DeVille of the Theatre Royal 6
Dickens, Charles 10
Dobbins, Guy 2
Dobells 35, 128
Dorwood, Helen 90, 99, 113
Doyle, John 87, 128, 131, 133, 136, 138-143
D'Oyly Carte 24, 29
Dresser, The 49
Driver, Betty 59
Drury Lane 3, 4, 5
Duchess Charles 129
Dyall, Valentine *85*, *90*, 91, *91*

E

Edwards, Nettie 143, 144, 149
Egyptian Hall, London 10, *10*
Elephant and Castle Theatre 15
Ellenborough Hotel 57, 67, 74, *74*, 75, 93

Elliott, William *158*, 159, 161
Ellis, Robin 96
English Wood Stage 18
Equity 95, 149, 150, 159, 163
Ervine, St. John 44
Evans, Carol 108, 115, 122-124, 136, 141, 151
EveryKid Club 155
Everyman Theatre Association (ETA) 77, 81, 82, 84, 85, 87, 100, 116, 151
Everyman Youth Theatre 140, 146, 147, 154, 156

F

Family Affair, A 146
Farquhar, Malcolm 35, 56, *63*, 101, 105-113, 115-117, *117*, 123, 128, 131, 136, 147
Ferrari, Fred 53
Festival of Youth 85
Fiddler on the Roof **140**, *141*
Final Daze 163
fire 15
Fitzhardinge, Lord 9
Fletcher, Cyril 56, *56*, *57*, 60, 105
Fontayne, Fine Time 144, 147
Foster, Tim *168*, 169, 170
Foster Wilson Architects 166, *166*, 169
Fox, Lee **113**
French, James John 125
French revues 57, 61, 73

G

Gardner, Joseph 5
Garrick, David 3, 49
Gatti, Jack 107
Gaunt, William 87, 90-92, *92*, 99, 105, 115
GCHQ 67, 81, 82, *82*, 89
Gebhard, Frederic 23

Gemson, Mick 133
ghosts 119-124
Gielgud, John 48, 55, 56, 127
Giles, David 76, 78, 99
Gill, Lucy **136**
Gill Smith, Cecil (Gillsmith) 28, 32
Gilmore, David 83, 93, 94, 96, 102, 129
Ginsbury, Norman 44
Glasgow 15
Gloucester 3, 4, 9, 38, 171
Glover, Julian 49
Grade, Lew and Leslie 59
Greening, Alison 141, 151, 155
Green Room 93, 128, 129, 141, 151
Gregory, Peter 102
Grenfell, Joyce 56
Grey, Edmund 103
Grimaldi, Joseph 5, *5*, 15
Grosvenor Terrace 3

H

Hackney Empire 15
Hadrian the Seventh 113
Hakim, Eric V. 41
Hall, Michael E. 143, 144, 155
Hammond, Rae 98, 103, 105-107, 109, 112, 123
Hancock, Stephen 91, 95, 113
Hardwicke, Edward 75
Harris, Rodney 86
Harvey, David **109**
Hasted, Michael 163
Hatherley Lawn 43
Heath, Monica 108
Hedda Gabler 108, 139
Hendry, Roger 107, 115, **118**, 121, 122, 124, 127, 128, 133, 136, 138, 142, 143
Hengler's Grand Cirque 15
Herbert, Dennis 59

Herford, Robin 156, **156**
Heritage Lottery Fund 167
Her Majesty's, Aberdeen 15
Hewlett, Donald 109
H.H. Martyn & Co. 97
High Street 2, 3, 5, 6, **8**, 15, 19, 35, 38, 91, 97
Hippodrome **31**, 32, 38
Hippodrome, London 15
Hodges, Peter 98
Hogan, James 102
Hogger, Richard 153
Holborow, John 39, 62
Holland, Wenda **139**
Hooray for Daisy **92**
Hopkins, Sir Anthony 146
Houghton, Martin 142-149
Howard, Alan 44
Howard, Arthur 44
Howell, Cllr. John 45
Hughes, Ray 120, 121
Hunt, Michael 149
Hunt, Martita 48
Hunter, N.C. 72
Hurt, John 105, 108, 110, 112, 115, 128, 136
Hyde, Mark 157, **158**, 161

I

Imperial Square 11, 32
Importance of Being Ernest 143, 144
Irving, Charles 68
It Ain't Half Hot Mum 76, 98, 109

J

Jacques, Hatti 55
Jam Tomorrow 154
Jane revue show **48**, 59, 61
Jane Eyre 146, 147
Jersey 23, 26
John Halifax, Gentleman 2

Johnson, Martin 85
Jones, Charlotte 63
Jones, Jeff 57
Jones, Nick 146, 147
Jones, Norman 91, **91**
Jones, Rachel 64
Jordan, Mrs. 3
Justice, Barry 98

K

Kay's Safety Bolt 18
Keith, Penelope 98
Kelly, Michael 2
Kelsey, David 91, **92**, 95
Kemble, John Phillip 2
Kennedy, Walter **109**
Kent, Barbara 43
King Edward VII 21
King George III 3, 4
King Lear 55, 98
King's School, Worcester 86
Knowles, Michael 109

L

Ladies' College 10, 42
Lady Clancarty 21, 23
Lady of Lyons, The 25
Laird, Peter **93**
Laine, Cleo 108, 138
Lancaster, Anthony 94
Langtry, Lillie 1, **20**, 21, 23-26, **26**, 135
Lapham, Miss 37
Leach, Rosemary 108-110, **108**
Leicester Theatre Royal 19
Leno, Dan 43
Lightstone, Jim 73
Lipson, Alderman D.L. 68
Lime-lights 59
Livesey, Roger 48
Lloyd, Arthur **30**, 31
Lloyd, Phyllida 138, 139
Lodge, Bubble 146

London Palladium 15
Lord Chamberlain 14, 97
Lotinga, Ernie 49, **52**
Lowe, Arthur 56
Lower Dockem 8
Lowrie, Philip 95
Lyndhurst, Nicholas 49
Lyric Hammersmith 15

M

Mabbett, Bryan 38
Macbeth 144, **145**
MacDonald, Stephen 86, 101
Mac, Jimmy 49, 51
MacKay, Angus 74, 75
MacKenzie, Sir Compton 43
Macready, William Charles 10, 11
Madame de Mundella (Catherine Wilson) 29
Maddox, Frank G. 41, 45, **62**, **63**, 64, 65
Maddox, Reg 41
Malcolm, Derek 65, 67
Man in Black, The 91
Mander, Sheila 139, 140, 143, 144, 154, 156
Mander, Kate 146
Maria Marten in the Red Barn 95, 96
Maskelyne, Jasper 10, 47
Maskelyne, John Neville **9**, 10, 47
Matcham, Frank **12**, 12-15, **15**, 18, 19, 21, 24, 25, 67, 73, 165, 170
Matthews, Jessie 62
Maxwell, Roberta 91, **93**
McBain, Robert 90-92, **90**, **92**
McCarthy, Lillah 22, **22**, 23, 27
McEwan, Tony **113**
McNeil, Miss Amy 25
Meet Your Friends 70, **72**

Metcalf, Roland 102
Metcalfe, Andy 171
Midland Theatre Company 64
Middlemas, Frank 96
Midsummer Night's Dream, A 37, 77
Milton, Paul 139, *139*, 142, 143, *161*, *161*, 163
Missy Malone *162*, 163
Mitton, Ruby 37
Monico, David 97
Montpellier 7, 10
Montpellier Chapter Hotel 7
Montpellier Gardens 38, 43
Moore, Roger 56
moratorium 78, 79, 112
Mort, Spencer 19
Mount, Peggy 109, *109*
Mullins, Ian 79, 83-85, 89-92, *90*, 94-96, 98, 99-101, 102, 103, 105, 107, 111-113, 116, 120, 147
My Fair Lady 133, 138

N

Napier Brown, Michael 111
Napier, Valantyne 57
National Theatre 102, 140, 146
Nelson, Harold B. 26
New Clarence Theatre 5
Newman, Noel 73, 77, 78, 84, *90*, 100, 103
New Royal Well **8**
New Theatre and Opera House 13, 16
Newton, Alfred W. 38
Niblett, Hilda 37
Nicholas, Paul 156, *156*
Nichols, Peter 98
Nicholls, Roger 81, 82, *82*, 89, 96, 99, 103
North Street 43, 44
Nossek, Ralph *76*, 91, *91*

Nude Shows 56, 57, 59, 60, 61, 62, 65
Nutmeg and Ginger 96

O

O'Callaghan, Tony 111
Old Royal Well Theatre 26
Old Well Pump Room 7
Old Mother Riley 51
Olivier, Laurence 48, 138
Onley, Samuel 7, 8
Opera House Cinema 41
Oriel Road 57, 67
Osborne, John 57, 64
Owen, Dudley 81, 82, 103, 112
Oxford Playhouse 73

P

Paganini 6, *7*
Page, Eileen 113
Paignton 14
Palmer, David 71
Pantomime 9, 45, 47, 49, 51, 55, 57, *62*, *79*, 105, 109, 128, *129*, 157, 159-161
Parish Church 2, 7
Parsons, John 61
Patel, Donald *see* Crosby
Pate's Grammar School 86
Pavilion, Montpellier Gardens 31, 38, 43
Pavlow, Muriel 48
Pearce, Michael *93*
Peel, Robert 26
Peer Gynt 131, 133, 138
Phillips, Captain Mark 108, 111, 138
Phillips, David 67, 68, 69, 75, 81, 115, 116
Pinter, Harold 74, 92
Pittville Pump Room 85
Pittville Street 2, 59
Playhouse, The 69, 87

Plough Hotel 6, *10*, 15, 22, 25, 27, 44, 59, 71, 127
Poeton, William 111
Ponsonby-Fane, Sir S. C. B. 14
Powell, Christopher 111, 115, 146
Powell, Peter 73, 75, 76, 78
Powell, Robert 172
Pre-Raphaelites 23
Prestbury 6, 43
Price, Amy *160*
Price, Hywel 94
Priestley Studios 71
Prince Albert Edward 23
Prince Henry School 86
Princess Anne 108, 138
Princess Hall, Ladies' College 10
Privates on Parade 98
Promenade 9, 19, 26, 35, 37, 52

Q

Queen Victoria 1, 23
Quilley, Denis 75

R

RADA 83
Rainger, Charles H. 125
Rainger, Herbert T. 32
Ramm, Zara *160*, 161
Rattigan, Terence 53, 55, 92
Ray, Andrew *75*
Raymond, Hugh 146
ReachOut 139, 140, 151, 161
Redford, H. Oswald 29, *29*, 33, 35
Redford, Robert 35
Regent Arcade 16, 127, *130*,
Regent Street 15, 19, 21, 26, 39, *39*, 44, 47, 91, 117, 129, 138, 172
Reid, Beryl 48
Repertory Theatre, North Street 43, 44

Reynolds, Dorothy 74-76, *76*, 96, *96*
Rhodes, Leslie *109*
Richardson, Ralph 48, 138, 155
Ridley, Arnold 48
Ridley, John 33, 79, 89, 90, *90*, 97, 98, 119
Robertson, Jean 120
Robinson, Hannah Maria 15
Robinson, Jethro 14, 15
Rodney Road 6
Rogers, Craig *136*
Rose, Clarkson 45, 51, 52, *79*
Rossignol, Signor 4
Rowe, Geoffrey 150, 159, *159*, 165, 166, 168, 169
Rowe, George 7
Royal Cinema de Luxe 43
Royal Old Well 7
Royalty Theatre, Glasgow 15
Royal Well Music Hall 7
Royal Well Theatre 9, 11

S

Sadler's Wells, London 5
Sadler's Wells, Cheltenham 5
Salad Days 70, 74, *88*, 91, 96, 107
Salberg, Derek 45, 62
Salberg, Keith, 45
Salberg, Reginald 45, 99
Salisbury Rep 45, 90, 91, 99
Salvation Army 8, 9
Sands, David 102
scagliola 18, *169*
Scotcher, Pamela 102
Scrivener, Jessie 42, 43
Secombe, Harry 56
Seward, Samuel 5
Shaw, George Bernard 21, 23
Shelley, Frank 65
Shipway, Bill and Ralph 49
Shipway-Blackwell, Nancy 49
Shirers & Lances 38

Siddons, Sarah 2, 3
Simpson, Richard *106*
Simpson, Wilfred 39, 41, 44, 45, 47, 49, 55, 62, 129
Singapore 43
Sir Thomas Rich School, Gloucester 86
Slade, Julian 70, 74, 83, 96
Slade/Reynolds 74, 91
Sleuth *110*, 111
Sloat (sliders and cuts) 19
Smith, Bernard *93*
Smith, Alderman P.T. 43
Smyth, Colonel 14
Solo 95, *97*
Sound of Music, The 143
speciality acts 55, 161
SpellerMetcalfe 170, 171
St. Clair-Ford, Captain 14
St. George's Place 5
St. James' Church 15
St. James' Square 38
St. Mary's Hall 69, 83
St. Peter's Hall 8
Stephens, Paula 146
Stroud 3
Studio Theatre 131, 133, 136, 138, 139, 140, 147, 155, 159, 161, 163
Sun Burner 17
Swinburne, Nora 48
Swift, William Thomas 9, 26

T

Tamburlaine the Great 89, 96
Taylor, Wink 123, 155, *155*, 161
Teague, J.M. 24, 25
Teal, Graham 45, 53
Tewkesbury 3
Tewkesbury Road 8
Tewson, Josephine 75, 84, 89, 90, *90*, 91, *91*, 93, 110, 111, 113, 119, 120

Theatre of Varieties 43
Theatre Royal 3, 4, *4*, 5, 6, 7, 125
Theatre Royal, Bath 41, 124
Theatre Royal, Montpellier 8
Theatre Royal, Newcastle 15, 159
Theatre Royal, Wakefield 19
Theatre*Search* 169
Theatre Week 84, 86, *86*
Thomson, Lionel 75, 91, *92*, 95, 119, 120
Tivoli Road 48
Town Hall 32, 51, 63, 101, 102, 113, 120, *129*, 128, 141
Turnham, Carol 141
Twelfth Night 141, 142
Twinkle 45, 51, *51*, 53

U

Ustinov, Peter 62

V

Vestibule, The 16, *17*, 35

W

Wade, Joan 108
Ward, Brian 57, 59, 60
Ward, Cllr. Edward 44
Waring, George *90*, 91, 105
Warner, John 96, *113*
Warwick Company of Comedians 2
Warwick Revue 43
Watson, John Boles 2-6, 125
Wellington, Duke of 5, 6
Wellington Hall 9
Wellington Square 11
Well Walk 7
Whelan, Robert 82, *84*, 91, 93, 95, *97*, 120, 124
Whistle Down the Wind 154
whistling 123
Whitehart Street 10

Whitestone, Derek 71
Wilde, Oscar 23, 55, 91
Wildest Dreams 74, 91, 103
Williams, Tudor 73, 155
Wilson Barrett Company 23
Wilson, Clarence 95
Windmill Theatre 45
Winter Gardens 11, *11*, 31, 32, 42-45
Winter Gardens Kinema 32
Winters, Bernie 57
Wolfit, Donald 49, 85, 96
Woman in Black, The 156, **157**
Wood, Cyril 69
Worcester 3, 4, 86, 136, 139
Worthington, Frank 25
Wright, Neal 146
Wynter, Mark *110*, 111

Y

York Hotel 5
York Passage 3, 5
YEG (Young Everyman Group) 71, 82-86, 80

Z

Zigger Zagger **141**